Bad B!tch
ON TOP

CONQUER YOUR
INNER GOOD GIRL IDENTITY
TO DOMINATE YOUR LIFE AND CAREER

Julia J. Cha

ISBN: 978-1-7770628-6-6

CONTENTS

CHAPTER ONE

Illusion

You've been living an illusion.

Y ou've been *good,* but your life isn't.

You feel lonely, burdened, and empty.

You deserve happiness, appreciation, and ease because all your life, you sacrificed and suffered from selflessness.

You've been living an illusion, and that's why you keep suffering.

You're defined by and exist for others.

This is why you're miserable.

You've been the Good Girl.

The opposite of the Good Girl is the Bad Bitch.

To be happy and fulfilled, this is who you have to become.

The Bad Bitch is a woman who gets what she wants.

When you make decisions that uplift *you* instead of others, those who project patriarchal expectations will inevitably label you as "bad" and call you "a bitch."

The Good Girl picks the path of least resistance.

She tries to become the Bad Bitch from time to time, but the minute she gets negative feedback, she drowns in guilt and shame, lets go of herself immediately, and becomes an even bigger pleaser.

The Bad Bitch picks the path of alignment.

When she's called "Bitch," she says, "Thanks" and owns the label.

The Good Girl lives by expectations.

She prioritizes making others happy and comfortable while sabotaging herself in the process.

She follows someone else's script for her life because it's "realistic."

She needs to make others happy so she won't feel lonely.

Sound familiar?

You were so focused on others all your life that you don't hear yourself anymore.

You've been so disconnected from yourself that you don't notice your self-sabotage until the harsh consequences hit you.

These consequences include losing your wealth, health, happiness, and missed opportunities.

Not to mention, losing the people you thought cared about you.

When you needed them the most, they disappeared.

You did everything right, yet they didn't take care of you.

They left, abandoned, and betrayed you.

And worst of all, you *betrayed yourself*, in the midst of being nice, looking happy, maintaining your outer image, and pleasing others.

As long as you continue to live focusing on other people, deprioritizing your desires and goals, and viewing the world through your rose-colored glasses, you will keep getting blindsided and hurt while never reaching your full potential.

From the moment you were born, you've been conditioned by patriarchy to become the Good Girl, to uphold the status quo, and to make everyone else's life easier.

The Good Girl is a pleaser, an addict to validation.

You were never seen, heard, and accepted for who you really are.

That's why when you get a little bit of affirmation or comfort, you get addicted to that source.

You have this addictive relationship with your boss, colleagues, lovers, family, and friends.

As a business owner, you're addicted to pleasing your clients, and even the professionals you hire.

This isn't your fault. It's *human nature*. Never caring about people's opinion isn't realistic because we're social animals, and we're wired for love and connection.

You're not "broken" or "damaged" for caring about what people think. As long as humans have existed, we have lived in tribes. We relied on social connection and support for survival. Isolation by exile was the worst punishment across all cultures in human history.

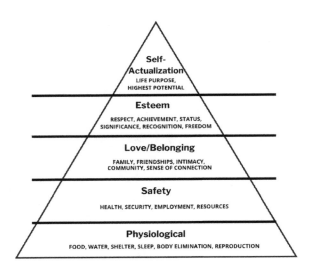

Maslow's Hierarchy of Needs

As Maslow's Hierarchy of Needs states, along with food, water, shelter, and basic income, *connection* is fundamental for our survival.

That's why you can't just cut people out.

That's why being alone feels like a death sentence.

You may think you have good connections, but actually, you're stuck in the third tier: Love and Belonging.

You've been surrounded by people, but you feel lonely because these relationships lack depth. What you have aren't authentic relationships.

They don't know you, and you don't really know them. This is true even for blood family, and people who you call your best friends.

You've been hanging onto whatever relationship you can get because you've been starved of real connection all your life. You had to please, nurture, and bend over backward to get your connection needs met by your family, peers, and then later, in the workforce.

You think that these inauthentic connections are how relationships are supposed to be.

They aren't.

You've been affection *starved* all your life, and that's why any type of validation swindles and sucks you in.

When you feel some sort of connection with someone, you lose all rhyme or reason.

You can't expect anyone who has been starved to choose food that is good for them, such as a healthy salad, over junk food, such as donuts or a big bacon cheeseburger.

It's logical that the more starved you are, the worse your food choices are going to be.

It's logical that the more starved you've been of healthy human connections in your upbringing, the worse your decision-making will be when it comes to choosing friends, lovers, and work cultures.

That's why you can't blame yourself for making a lifetime of bad decisions and settling, with lower pay than what you deserve, overworking, keeping yourself small, and allowing in lovers, family, and friends who barely show up to reciprocate your efforts.

You can't blame yourself for feeling addicted to someone who used you, betrayed you, and broke your heart.

You can't blame yourself for giving them so many last chances and the benefit of the doubt that they didn't deserve, wth your hope inflating at the slightest sign of their redemption, which they used to maintain the status quo.

Being smart doesn't protect you from this trap. You keep doing this even when you've read a lot of books, hold high degrees, and have a good job. When you look at the Hierarchy of Needs, until you resolve the Love and Belonging tier, you can't become significant and achieve your highest potential.

That's why you want more, but you're stuck.

The Love and Belonging needs are primitive. The unmet needs are controlling every aspect of your decision-making, both in your personal life and business.

Your primitive desires are controlled by your subconscious mind, your deepest emotions.

The emotions below your level of conscious awareness rule your habits. Willpower doesn't stand a chance.

Up to 97% of the reason why you decide is based on emotions. Only the remaining 3% is based on logic. What you choose is based on the feeling of familiarity because this gives you comfort.

Familiarity *feels* safe, even when it isn't safe.

That's why you do things, and you don't know why you do them. You have recurring patterns and problems. You make decisions then use your logic to justify why.

That's why you can't think your way out of unhappiness, dissatisfaction, and recurring problems.

That's why you can't be expected to *know better* when it comes to making sabotaging decisions.

You're used to dealing with your negative feelings by chasing pleasure.

Your life is so stressful that you have to indulge every so often to *take the edge off*.

Yet, no amount of designer handbags or shoes can ever solve your Good Girl problem.

Another getaway to Paris, France, feels good, but it deepens your burnout.

The more you try to fix your life with the Good Girl mindset, the worse it gets for you.

A bigger income, a more luxurious house, a more accomplished partner, and even a gaggle of kids won't nourish your depleted, dreary, and desiccated spirit.

Instead, these types of "expansions" suck you dry even more because, in the process, you become a robotic shell of a being, existing in service of others.

You ask, "What's wrong with me?"

It's the same question that an addict asks when they have a moment of sobriety.

Just like an addict, that moment of clarity does not last long, as long as you keep *taking the edge off*.

That euphoria from validation is so strong that you are blind to the patterns when they're unfolding.

You can't stop to reflect because facing reality is too painful.

An addict lives for the high of her next hit.

The Good Girl lives for the next high from validation.

An addict suffers from withdrawal.

The Good Girl suffers from loneliness.

An addict does anything to get the next hit.

The Good Girl does anything to beg for more attention, including becoming a more sophisticated pick-me to shapeshift to gain validation.

As a modern woman born, bred, and raised in patriarchy, your mind is crowded with unhelpful and impossible expectations and standards.

You feel compelled to please and to follow instructions.

In patriarchy, a grown woman is permanently treated like a child. She is infantilized. She gets validation when she looks young and acts like a child. This is the societal standard for feminine beauty, the standard that is the root of insecurity in every modern woman walking this Earth.

She's trained to live an unfulfilling life where she keeps herself small and dependent on others. For example, when she quits her job erratically or makes a bad decision, she always has a boyfriend, a husband, or parents' arms to run into.

The Good Girl fights an impossible expectation that she expires after 30, indicating that an older woman has no value in society. No matter how powerful she believes she is, she's evaluated by the patriarchal standard that matches her worth to her ability to breed. The obsession with staying young eternally devalues her experience and wisdom, which can only be embodied with time and aging.

This patriarchal force is so pervasive that a woman's existential crisis is rooted in this subconscious force and an unconscious bias for her to force youthfulness, which in turn becomes a self-imposed self-sabotage to *stay naïve*.

Your naïveté is thinking that you can play all the same patriarchal expectations and become a rich, successful boss lady who dominates in an important line of work.

Your fantasy is simply role-playing success, where you're successful while being everything patriarchy approves of.

This expectation is unrealistic and rooted in naïveté. While you're juggling to do it all, you harm your health and wellness, while you lose your identity as an individual.

You experience Stockholm syndrome where you fall in love with your oppressor, the very system that guarantees that you'll fail in your desire for happiness, freedom, and autonomy. You will self-destruct as soon as you see any form of tangible success.

As soon as the Good Girl is successful, the other shoe drops.

Your naïveté gets the best of you. Your family and friends become leeches. You trust the wrong person. You are betrayed. Money flows in and out, as fast as it comes in.

You can't help this.

Your mind has been programmed through your childhood experiences and observations.

When you say to yourself, "I'll never be helpless or be treated like mom/aunt/grandma," you fall exactly into this trap. You have been programmed since birth by their stories, and that means you are doomed to walk into relationships that will deplete and use you just the same way.

You've been conditioned by societal expectations, Disney movies, rom-coms, and K-Dramas to live in a fantasy where you're made to believe that if you act to meet the patriarchal standards, you will succeed as the chosen one.

Like Ariel, you give up your voice.

Like Lara Croft, you have to be sexy but act like a man to be cool and powerful.

Like Hermione, you get to be a boy's smart sidekick, but not the hero. You save the day, but you never get to be the real main character.

When you're successful, you feel chosen. You think you beat the system, but the truth is quite the contrary.

Being chosen is fitting into a world that centers on men.

No matter how much you say you believe in yourself, you still dream of the day that a man will save you from a huge problem or at least will fetch you and give you your happily ever after.

When you think this way, you're far from *beating* the system.

Girls and women believe in the Disney princess stories over the real-life warnings from accomplished women who perished due to patriarchal forces.

Princess Diana, a real-life *good* princess, seemed to be living the ultimate dream life of marrying the prince of the most powerful monarchy in the world. Her life was far from idealistic. She was allegedly cheated on, defamed, and met an early death. She was ruined by patriarchal forces.

Britney Spears was a talented and accomplished woman who *made it* so young, at only 16 years old, and held down the title of "Princess of Pop" even after almost a decade of being inactive. She *had it all* but was ultimately exploited and ruined by patriarchy. According to her, her father controlled and used her, her family followed suit, every man she had ever been with exploited her, and the patriarchal court system unjustly enabled the ongoing abuse.

man will not lead you to your Promised Land. This secret desire, even when you're living an independent life, is your Achilles' heel.

ou feel this desire because this is what you were conditioned to ant. Even as you reach heights, your mind will remain susceptible o succumbing to this weakness.

ecoming the Bad Bitch requires you to become wise, and that eans you have to learn from the mistakes of those who preceded ou, rather than thinking that their challenges are not relevant to ou or that you've somehow outsmarted the system as an excep- onal prodigy.

ou think you beat the system, but as long as you run on a checklist f never-ending responsibilities that involve caretaking, endlessly roviding, and doing emotional labor for others, you keep up the ycle of self-oppression.

ou turn to self-development, and while that does help you, it's not nough. Your patriarchal mindset, people's unconscious biases, nd our societal system are the invisible forces chokeholding you, eeping you from making further progress. It's like trying to climb a ountain with chains attached to your body.

s a woman boss, being a leader is much harder than you thought would be.

nding a guy seemed so easy for so many women you've known, et this simple task feels impossible.

turns out, earning is the easiest part of money, and money man- gement is harder than you ever imagined.

ie Good Girl keeps asking, "What's wrong with me?"

ut this is the wrong question. It doesn't address the thousands of ears of patriarchy and the oppressive mental conditioning that, no matter how much you try to *make it work,* designated you to choose a path of unhappiness.

As long as you keep asking the wrong question, you'll never move forward. To get the right answer, you need to ask the right question.

The right question is "What will it *actually* take?"

You never stopped to think that the self-development that you've been religiously following was developed by privileged white men who wanted more privilege.

In other words, while those books were helpful, they were not written for someone like you, being of a different gender, race, or even economic class, being someone who the world doesn't naturally want to give credit to or look up to as a leader.

None of those books address your Good Girl mental programming, the root cause of all your problems.

The Good Girl's glass ceiling is a combination of self-sabotaging naïveté and habits, combined with the unconscious biases and expectations of others who immediately disregard your authority and competence.

Nothing will motivate you to break out of the painful cycle perpetuated by the illusion until you experience the greatest reality check i.e., heartbreak.

This heartbreak is what novelists call the Dark Night of the Soul.

It's when your illusion-based life disintegrates before your eyes.

You lose your loved ones and see the true faces of your friends.

You lose money, your health, and your sanity.

You no longer even love the career you worked hard for.

You lose hope as the life you worked so hard for crumbles around you.

At this point, you have three choices:

1. Stay down and barely survive.

2. Try to rebuild the same way, which will only lead you here again in the future.

3. Start again from scratch, doing it the right way, and *doing what it takes*.

What is the way forward when you've been a Good Girl all your life? Is there another way to be?

There is. And that's what I'm going to share with you now.

The Bad Bitch is a phoenix that rose from the Good Girl's ashes.

She's the authentic essence remaining when the Good Girl's patriarchal conditioning is questioned to such a deep level and burned down to nothingness.

This is the process where you figure out who you really are, since up until this point your entire personality has been coping mechanisms and patriarchal brainwashing.

So, who are you, really?

You're your True Self as the Bad Bitch. You no longer make other people comfortable because you don't abide by their standards.

As wonderful as this sounds, you have to be ready to face tremendous counterforces.

People notice your changes and call you a *bitch*.

People gossip, write anonymous negative reviews about you, and exclude you from their community.

This is where the Good Girl caves.

The Bad Bitch is powerful because she's woken up from the illusion.

- ◆ She alchemizes the hate to become more self-assured and assertive.
- ◆ She prioritizes herself and the goals that matter to her.
- ◆ She ruthlessly lets go of what doesn't fit into her agenda.
- ◆ She is a master of human motivation and behavior.
- ◆ She protects herself from the unconscious biases of others in her dealings.
- ◆ She uses her resourcefulness and social mastery to create the life she wants.
- ◆ She always looks glamorous to the world, but the transformation is more than what meets the eye.

It's a process of many growth spurts, transitions, and pivots while being dedicated to a specific purpose.

You can't be happy, successful, and fulfilled until you become the Bad Bitch.

Nothing you want in life will come to fruition until you recognize the illusions, shed the harmful patriarchal programming, and become who you really are meant to be.

This book is about transitioning from being the Good Girl to the Bad Bitch so you can *thrive* as a leader, experience true happiness in your human experiences, and succeed in your life's work.

To embrace this change, you must be willing to be radically honest and shine a light on every hidden shadow and crevice of your thoughts and patterns.

You change your mindset.

You change your habits.

You become an expert in the laws of power.

You become an expert in human motivation.

You embody sophisticated social elegance to get what you want and to have doors open for you.

You must build a supportive community that elevates you beyond what you can do alone.

Instead of unconsciously being played, you understand the rules, and play to win.

All those years of looking for an answer to your happiness, fulfillment, wealth, and love, this is the exact transformation that you needed all along.

This is *doing what it takes*.

CHAPTER TWO

Ambition

The catalyst for the Bad Bitch journey.

The Bad Bitch is the Good Girl who started *doing what it takes.* Ambition is the catalyst.

Ambition is what sets the Good Girl and the Bad Bitch apart and what begins the transformation journey.

The Good Girl has an oppressed mindset, so she doesn't feel good enough to own her ambition.

Doing what it takes to become happy and successful involves becoming significant outside of the family role as a daughter, sister, mother, or wife.

It involves you being seen, heard, and highly celebrated for showcasing your competence, intelligence, speech, performance, or artistry.

It involves you becoming influential and powerful in your professional arena.

When the Good Girl realizes that she has great ambitions, she feels guilt and shame and usually goes through a long contemplation period.

She tells herself she doesn't know what to do or where to start, but deep down, she does know.

She's overcome by a lot of self-doubt, so it feels safer to pretend like she doesn't know what she wants.

It's easier for you to lie to yourself because the grandiosity of it is too overwhelming.

That's why it's easier for the Good Girl to stay ignorant of her own ambitions.

It's easier for you to have big dreams but play small.

"Who do you think you are?" is what follows you everywhere in your head.

These words put you down. They convince you to stop believing in yourself, even when things are working out or when the circumstances are right for you to start now, you don't see them. You can't keep going. You think you should stop or do it later.

These words are not your own words.

They are your parents, family, culture, and even your lovers, which now, you mistakenly think that these words are your own.

You think that these words are "reality" and "the absolute truth."

You have the desire to become significant and successful, yet these words don't allow you.

You're stuck.

That's why instead of following your own dreams, you focus on helping others achieve their dreams.

You pretend to be happy where you are.

You pretend that you don't really want so much wealth, recognition, or accolades.

You stay chaotic and mediocre.

You don't want to offend someone by becoming successful.

You punish yourself.

You overwork, overgive, and diminish your sense of self.

This is how the Good Girl wastes years and even decades of her life not doing much at all.

It's the life of an addict, full of extreme highs and lows, but it's on autopilot. It is boring.

The Good Girl needs a reality check in the form of a harsh lesson.

She needs to fail badly to wake up.

This can be getting cheated on, getting divorced, fired, betrayed, sick, or having a midlife crisis.

You need to experience the death of an era through your current hardship.

That's where the Dark Night of the Soul comes in. This existential crisis wipes your reality clean and shows you that your hopes and dreams were nothing but an illusion, shaped by other people's expectations of you.

There is nobody else but yourself that you can count on, and now you know that.

There is nobody but you who can save you.

There is nobody but you who can protect your values, family, and heirs.

You have nothing to live for unless you find your own purpose to live for.

Under the chaos and pressure of an existential crisis, the Good Girl cracks, but in between that crack, a flower starts to bloom.

You recognize that there is a Self within you, and within that Self, there is a fire.

That fire is your ambition.

Knowing your ambition is like knowing yourself.

Honoring your ambition is the greatest self-respect and self-validation.

Your existential crisis is telling you, between tears, anguish, and loss of hope, that *it's time.*

This is your chance. It's now or never.

For the first time in your life, you feel *courage* to acknowledge your ambition and to take action.

Ambition is what gets you to think about who you really are, what your purpose is, and what will truly fulfill you.

The pathway to fulfilling your ambition is a spiritual process.

When you start to take action for yourself, you awaken.

Waiting to "awaken" will not work.

This awakening becomes a sense of urgency to take action and to stay consistent.

When courage from finding your ambition and the urgency to make it happen start to meld, this is where you start your Bad Bitch transformation.

If the Good Girl is a caterpillar, then Bad Bitch is the butterfly.

This in-between awakening, the *courage* stage, is the chrysalis.

The metamorphosis isn't as simple as just growing wings while being hidden inside the cocoon.

The caterpillar dissolves inside the cocoon until only her essence remains, and with that, nature reconstructs her into a butterfly.

When you tap into your courage, the process of finding your ambition is simple.

1. **Reflect** on what skills and talent you have gotten positive feedback on from those who weren't even invested in your success.

   For example, reflect on the times when strangers complimented you on a project or a creation or when someone extremely picky acknowledged your talent.

   If you have gotten paid, or have been offered payment in exchange for your talent or skill, you're definitely on the right track.

2. **Feel** your body when you practice those skills and talents.

   We naturally love what we're good at and feel passion for it. When your specific skill and talent are highly coveted by others, and you feel elated when practicing it, then you're definitely on the right track.

3. **Envision** in detail what your life would be like, and how you'd feel in that life, doing that work every single day. This is your purpose.

   This is what drives the initial motivation and gives you the energy and the urgency to take action.

4. **What It Takes** to make your ambition come to fruition isn't obvious in the beginning.

    Start clarifying what privileges and advantages you already have to get started, then hire a mentor or a coach to identify some of the gaps and improvements you may need. Work towards polishing your strength and learning other skills you need to make it happen.

5. **Speak** boldly about your legacy, the type of change you're here to create in this world with your gift and talent.

    The more you speak, the more you make yourself accountable, and the more urgency and motivation you feel.

When you get started on your ambition, you realize that you should have started sooner.

This is true for everyone.

Today is the next best time to start since five years ago.

The more you take action, the more competent and confident you become, and the more the sense of urgency builds.

You start where you are, and as you progress, you train your character to become more resourceful, assertive, action-taking, and self-assured.

When you start living your ambition, from a chrysalis living in limbo, you complete your metamorphosis to become a butterfly.

You become that Bad Bitch.

THE BAD BITCH WHO BUILT AN EMPIRE

Born in 1867 in Louisiana as a black woman to previously enslaved parents, Sarah Breedlove had barely any statistical chance to amount to anything in racially hostile and divided America. After losing her mother at an early age, she went to live with her sister, where she suffered violence from her brother-in-law. To escape his abuse, she got married at 14. From that marriage, she had a daughter named A'Lelia.

Her abusive husband died in 1887 when her daughter was two years old.

Her courageous phase began when she committed to making enough money to make sure that her daughter got an education so she could have a better life. Sarah worked as a laundress, making less than a dollar a day.

Sarah lived the challenges of every black woman during her time, facing constant abuse and lack of opportunities under racial and gender oppression, with the added challenge of being a single mother. Sarah married again for the second time in 1894, but that marriage led to more disappointment and ended in a divorce, which was looked down on at that time, especially for the woman.

During this time, Sarah met Annie Malone, a hair care entrepreneur who sold hair products to black women via mail order. After hundreds of years of mistreatment, dehumanization, and abuse, any type of self-care for black women was revolutionary. With the end of slavery, black people finally had financial ability, making them eligible customers, yet their needs were still being largely ignored as a customer demographic.

Sarah initially did demo sales for Annie's hair product. It quickly became evident that Sarah had a huge knack for sales and entrepreneurship. She told the story of how she used to suffer from dandruff as her hair was falling out and using the product made her hair grow healthy and quickly, which built her self-esteem. She tied hair care to increasing confidence and making elevating decisions in her life, such as becoming confident and courageous to learn to choose herself in the midst of being in a disrespectful and abusive relationship. Her story drew in black women customers in the masses.

All her customers, including Sarah herself, wanted the same thing: to be and feel beautiful, increase their confidence, and have financial power and independence.

This gave Sarah a new purpose and an idea to start her own hair care and product business that met all three purposes. She created her own hair product, which she sold by telling her story and doing free hair demos on women. She later opened a retail store with a salon attached to it to do the hair demos in the same space as the retail store, to give the women the experience of being high-value. She hired and trained saleswomen on how to use the products and do the demos. This created a huge network of motivated, commission-based saleswomen who started growing the company exponentially. Her business became a *movement*.

As the leader of this movement, Sarah rebranded herself by giving herself a new name: Madam C. J. Walker.

"Madam" was a French title that addressed high-ranking and successful women in some African-American communities. Renaming herself gave her brand credibility and trust by associating her with elegance and sophistication.

C. J. Walker was the name of her third husband. In a strictly patriarchal society, Sarah had to play by those rules, while the marriage ended in divorce as Sarah became more successful. Her husband wasn't able to grow his mindset to treat her with importance. He betrayed Sarah with one of her salespersons. He later attempted to sabotage Sarah by creating a competitor hair care line with his mistress. Their attempts were unsuccessful. Sarah's passion, originality, business acumen, and commitment to her ambition weren't easily thwarted by menial jealousy. Sarah believed and worked for a greater purpose and legacy. They did not.

Sarah the Bad Bitch never remarried.

Her business quickly reached multi-million status in just a few short years.

Sarah Breedlove started out as the Good Girl working menial jobs, conditioned to play small as she was abused and oppressed by systemic racism, patriarchy, and generational trauma.

Sarah's commitment to provide for her daughter gave her the courage to start her initial Bad Bitch journey. Putting herself out there doing sales became the catalytic initiation. Her Madam identity was her Bad Bitch unleashing. Her divorcing from a man who betrayed her was her basking in Bad Bitch glory.

Her journey uplifted others. Her business was a huge success as her products gave African-American women a means to meet their deepest desires and needs: financial independence, a strong sense of worth, and a purpose in life to become significant.

Until her death in 1919 at the age of 51, Sarah was relentless in philanthropic initiatives. She was highly active as a patron of the arts. She is notable for providing a gathering place for African-American community leaders in Harlem.

She made sure her legacy lived through her daughter, A'Lelia. She passed on her business and wealth to her daughter, and her empire continued on as a matrilineal legacy.

This determined Good Girl defied all odds and generational trauma to build an extraordinary Bad Bitch empire, driven by ambition, purpose, and a desire for a lasting legacy. She defied all odds to become one of the first women in American history to achieve millionaire status.

CHAPTER THREE

Faith

Faith is the miracle maker.

Pursuing any type of great ambition takes you down an off-the-beaten path, and that pathway is nothing but uncertainty ahead.

There is no such thing as an exact template for reaching success.

There are certainly general trends and guidelines, but no guarantee about how and when it will happen for you.

This is why every Bad Bitch is spiritual.

She is fueled by *faith*.

Faith is having complete trust and confidence in the unknown.

You don't have to know how, you just have to start.

You don't have to have the guarantee that this particular method will be what makes it happen, you just have to give it a go.

The Bad Bitch takes action regardless of what happens, despite the fear of failure and unmet expectations.

The Good Girl doesn't have faith; she has *hope*.

Just like an addict runs on drugs, Good Girls run on hope; hope that magic will one day save her, that divine intervention will happen, or that some higher power will part the water in front of her and tell her, "It's time for you to begin."

Hope is *esperanza* in Spanish, rooted in Latin *sperare*. *Esperanza* comes from the word *esperar*, which means to wait.

This is why hope is dangerous.

You wait for signs to begin.

You wait to feel less fear.

You wait for someone to save you.

You wait until it feels better or it feels more convenient.

You run on hope, and that's why you're forever waiting.

While you wait on your ambition, you wait in service to others.

Your default response for anything that gives you progress is, "I have to think about it."

The Good Girl daydreams while she waits and falsely believes that the grandiose success and happiness she sees in her mental vision is her future destiny.

In reality, she procrastinates because she's terrified.

She's afraid of change because she's afraid of every outcome possible, of failing, feeling like a beginner, looking stupid, being embarrassed, being talked about, and being seen as an underachiever.

She's afraid of success.

She's afraid of jealousy from others.

She's afraid of criticism and judgment.

Her biggest fear of all is when she succeeds, she won't be seen as a good person anymore.

Then she will be alone, and she's afraid of loneliness. That's why she can't bet on herself. She can't disappoint people.

She does what feels safe. Instead of focusing on her ambition, she chooses to watch it play out in her imagination and convinces herself that one day she'll live an exciting life.

Hope is the reason why you keep contemplating your ambition while never helping yourself.

You help others, which is focusing externally, so you can avoid focusing inward because focusing inward requires you to become radically honest with your fears.

So, you keep yourself busy while hopefully waiting.

You focus on work that doesn't mean much to you because you're afraid of being let down.

Hope is how you already lost decades of your life, tens of thousands of dollars in a scam, and how you missed every God-given chance to turn your life around.

Hope is your comfort zone, your enabler, your enemy.

Hope is a liar that is stealing your future.

Faith is the nurturer, supporter, and lover that helps you overcome the fear so you can move into progress.

The Bad Bitch is faithful to herself and her mission.

Nobody can make you succumb to faith. That's your personal choice. This surrender can be the one thing keeping you away from your Bad Bitch initiation.

Many movers and shakers of the world were born into a disadvantaged socioeconomic environment and were told by others that they'd never amount to anything. Think Maya Angelou, Dolly Parton, and Malala Yousafzai.

But they knew they would, and they did.

Faith is simple yet powerful.

Faith is what fuels the Bad Bitch to overcome her fears, to start, and to play her cards right, no matter what cards she's been dealt.

Every Bad Bitch believes that she's already been chosen, given an advantage, and she's the one to create her impact in this world.

She takes the steps needed to achieve this destiny.

The Good Girl's hope involves waiting for external forces to take control of her issues to give her a magical outcome. Frequently this involves being saved by a man or being discovered, much like winning a lottery.

When it doesn't happen, the truth crashes around her and she turns to toxic positivity to self-soothe.

She tells herself some story that she's too high vibrational for people to understand her or that she's too special to thrive in this world.

After part-timing on her ambition for some time, the Good Girl quits and conforms to the societal norm.

However, the Bad Bitch is just getting started.

Hope didn't work out for you, if it did, you wouldn't be here, so it's time to embody *faith*.

The faithful Bad Bitch is an unstoppable force of nature.

She doesn't know how, but she'll figure it out.

She trusts herself because she's already come this far.

She believes that she's the creator, the alchemist, and the leader meant to make an impact.

She is backed by her ancestral spirits to be the one to renew the generational line.

She is backed by a lifelong legacy where she will become who she's required to become to serve her purpose as a change-maker.

Her energy and motivation are based on this deep trust in herself.

Her energy is magnetic.

She oozes competence, confidence, and humbleness.

Her sense of knowing, commitment, and determination opens doors and impresses the right people.

She's an unrealistic yet realistic phenomenon that beats every odds.

Embody faith, because Faith is the Bad Bitch's middle name.

Faith Made This Bad Bitch a Millionaire

I often get many Facebook friend requests which I ignore, but this one hit differently. Her profile photo was of a young black woman in a bright red dress speaking on a stage. Her photo radiated powerful energy.

When I spoke to her, I felt more excitement than ever. I often think of my profession as a coach being a part of global Star Search, and I knew from the moment I met her that Eno Eka was a star. I immediately felt her potential as a powerful influencer and entrepreneur. She was impressive.

Only two years before, Eno had moved from Nigeria to Canada by herself. While she worked as a business analyst, she created a training program that helped many others get into six-figure business analysis careers like her. Her expedited program trained people without tech degrees in business analysis to help them get hired by prestigious companies within six months.

Her program was so effective that she wanted to take a chance on entrepreneurship. Her faith had led her to invest in different types of business studies. She learned about online training school businesses and built her training program.

She looked for a coach who could help her dial in and accelerate her entrepreneurship. We started with a three-month contract working together.

As I got to know her better, it was evident that Eno had a history of being fueled by faith.

Nothing came easy for her. She came from Nigeria with only enough money to survive for two weeks due to the currency conversion from Naira to Canadian Dollars. She desperately needed a job. The immigrant community, her new support system, told her that no matter what her expertise was, she should take any menial job because the chances of getting a tech job as a newcomer were little to none.

Eno had faith that she deserved a business analysis job. She deserved to work in her profession. She refused to get a job as a cleaner, carer, warehouse stocker, customer service representative, or in retail, as many professional immigrants immediately cave under the pressure of needing a job. She experienced a lot of scrutiny and judgment from helpful people when she shared that she wasn't going to apply to these downgraded jobs.

She didn't know how, but with only faith by her side, she figured it out, step by step. She took training and tutorials on how to make her resume appealing and excel in interviews. After applying for approximately a hundred jobs within those two weeks, she landed a job in business analysis. She got started, then upgraded her career again, and within nine months of being a new immigrant, she had a six-figure job, had a dream home, her dream car, and was living her dream life.

Faith made it happen for her, even at the most trying times.

With entrepreneurship, Eno's new challenge was needing to level up her faith.

We set a date to quit her day job six weeks from the moment we started our coaching relationship to fully transition into entrepreneurship.

Faith works in strange ways.

As the day to quit her job approached, she got a promotion.

That wasn't all. The COVID quarantine started at the same time.

This is how the Universe tests you.

She didn't know how she'd do it, but she saw herself as the CEO of a training school that changed thousands, if not millions, of lives.

With faith and commitment to her purpose, she quit her job.

Six months later, her training school reached a quarter million dollars and produced hundreds of students getting incredible job results.

She wasn't just helping them get a job. She was helping many of them break their financial generational curses.

Eno's business reached multi-million dollars, and she is the CEO of this popular training school.

Eno Eka is now recognized as a celebrity in her community and was awarded the 2022 Canada's Most Powerful Women: Top 100™ Award.

She had nothing but uncertainty ahead of her, and in many pivotal moments of her journey, anxiety consumed her and made her future seem bleak. Faith gave her the energy, motivation, and creativity to find solutions and leverage the right types of people.

Faith made her a millionaire.

Faith helped her achieve the impossible, as there is a 4% chance of becoming a millionaire in Canada and much less chance as a brand-new immigrant.

Faith is what creates every miracle.

CHAPTER FOUR

Power Words

Words change your life.

The words in your mind can make or break you.

You see a vision and *feel* based on those words.

Based on those feelings, you're driven to take action.

You move toward what gives you pleasure and move away from pain.

The actions that you practice over and over again become your habit.

Your habit, over time, feels like your personality.

The Good Girl has a self-deprecating habit because of her choice of words.

You believe that you're confident until turning your ambition into reality proves to be hard.

"I'm *just* me in my corner doing my best."

"*Maybe* I can become successful, rich, and famous."

"I *guess* I'm pretty good at what I do."

Your uncertain words reflect your less-than identity. You're sorry to talk highly of yourself, even in your own mind. That's why you play small.

You believe that your thoughts are reality, when in fact, your reality is a reflection of your words.

The Bad Bitch takes control of her thoughts. She embodies success habits because she is intentional.

"I'm here to conquer with my personal best."

She does her personal best and won't stop until she does. She goes hard and gives it a little more as extra gravy.

"I'm committed to finding out my potential because of how dissatisfied I'd be to die without knowing."

She has a sense of urgency to make it happen now, not tomorrow.

"Fucking hell, I'm the best at this! I'm a powerhouse!"

She's excited to take on a bigger and better project or client to grow her reputation or to take on a bigger promotion.

The Good Girl doesn't pause to consider the words in her mind and instead blurts them out.

She speaks from disempowerment and uncertainty, which invites disrespect and dismissal.

Instead of owning something remarkable you did, you are afraid to come across as a show-off, so you humble yourself and say, "Oh, it's *just a little* business I started."

You're making $5,000, $8,000, or $100,000 a month in that *little* business, but you keep minimizing your success.

You dethrone yourself as the expert. "I *think* I know the answer."

You have an equivalence of a Ph.D. in your area of expertise, yet you still speak like this.

I once worked with a Good Girl client who told me that she didn't have many successes. She thought that by this age, she should be in a C-level position. She maintained that while she was pretty successful in the oil and gas industry, being the only female in every room, she didn't like where she was, so she didn't think much about herself.

When we dug in deep, she had done remarkable things. She flew in helicopters, made life-and-death decisions for others, and even negotiated with a prime minister in a European country in regards to their aviation law so her company could fly their helicopters over that country's sky, as needed.

She was a powerhouse, yet she hid her light.

Her perceived problem was that she didn't feel respected by her peers and boss.

Her actual problem was the words in her mind. "I'm not much," "I'm not where I want to be," and therefore, "I'm not good enough."

She was "Meh" in her mind, and that's how she presented herself.

The Good Girl is not aware of the impact of her words and how that translates into her actions.

You downplay your success and worth.

You tell yourself you're not enough, so you settle in a relationship, in your salary, while overdelivering.

You feel resentful and undervalued by others, without realizing that you allowed this to happen to yourself.

When you sense people depreciating your value, you desperately attempt to win them back by oversharing.

You start pumping yourself up, talking too much, which comes across as desperate.

In a desperate attempt to prove your worth, you go to the opposite extreme with great effort.

The Good Girl's thinking process is binary; it's either black or white.

She's either good or bad, successful or unsuccessful, and people are either for her or against her.

That's where you escalate to overblown self-importance: "I'm better than them! I can't let them dim my light!"

You inflate yourself and go over the top.

In that process, you shut people down, don't make space for others, and dim their light so you can be the only one who shines.

This is how you completely lose people.

Your words perpetuate an anti-connection, anti-leadership, and anti-happiness reality.

Your words can empower or disempower you, as well as the people around you.

The Bad Bitch takes control of the words in her mind and uses them to build her future.

She is impeccable with her words because words hold power, and she knows this.

She always thinks twice before speaking, posting on social media, and taking a stance.

Once she makes a decision to publicize her words, she is certain and concise.

Once she speaks, she has thought about it for a while.

She equally takes the words in her own mind seriously. They can make or break her.

Even the most accomplished Bad Bitch has moments of disempowering words.

When the moment comes for her to put a financial number to her skills, knowledge, and experience, she can feel a moment of doubt about her worth.

"If I charged less, would I be happy to deliver and care for this job/client?"

Quality in her life and work is her integrity, and therefore, she chooses wisely. She prices herself fairly.

The Bad Bitch feels the words before she says them.

"I'm not good at this" immediately makes her feel low, so she chooses, "I'm learning and progressing. Look at all the tangible upgrades I made today." These words feel empowering and motivating.

The Good Girl says, "There's no one who looks like me at that table." These words make her want to give up. The Bad Bitch chooses, "I'm here to be an example for others who need to see someone like me at that table."

The Good Girl says, "I just need this to be easier," which makes the milestone harder and the goal hard to reach. The Bad Bitch chooses, "What skill do I need to learn and improve to succeed?"

The right words that she says to herself propel the Bad Bitch forward. They motivate and encourage her. When she starts seeing results, she celebrates by bringing that progress to the limelight, and it gives her more faith.

The words that she says earn her respect.

The words she says to you makes you love her. She's addictive because even just hearing her words makes you feel your potential.

Empowerment is contagious, and it all starts with the right choice of words in your mind.

Ready to create a Bad Bitch reality? Here's how:

1. **Awareness** that your thoughts and words are not a predictor of the future. You must choose your thoughts and words carefully to lift you out of self-doubt, dependency, sabotage, doom, and torture.

2. **Choose** the right words that elevate you and direct you toward what you want and you'll drive towards the outcome that you want.

3. **Gather Positive Feedback** by taking note of positive changes after taking uplifting, congruent actions.

4. **Confirmation** that this change of word was better for your survival and thriving.

5. **Repeat** thoughts and actions that are congruent with the desired outcome to make empowering growth your default automatic habit.

Every successful person uses the power of words to focus, achieve daunting tasks under pressure, and to stay driven, energized, and motivated.

Tennis player Coco Gauff was interviewed about the pressure of being an elite top player. At only 19 years of age, she had won the 2023 US Open.

She said, "...at first I used to think negative things like why is this so much pressure? Why is this so hard?... in a way it's pressure, but it's not. I mean there's people struggling to feed their families. There's people who don't know where the next meal is gonna come from. There's people who have to pay their bills, and that's real pressure. That's real hardship. That's real life... I'm in a very privileged position. I'm getting paid to do what I love and getting support to do what I love." - Interview at the US Open.

It's not a wild guess to say that Coco's words shape her perspective and her reality. Instead of seeing her position as a world-class athlete as pressure and hardship, she sees it as a privilege that she needs to be grateful for. Her mind says, "This is easy because look how hard other people have it." Playing world-class isn't hard or stressful for Coco. She does her personal best on what she does best.

I tell my clients, those who find themselves in a slump or feeling down from business challenges, similar words to elevate their mindset.

I once had an entrepreneur client who was going on a rant about being sick of being on social media as an introvert. She just wanted her business to make money without her participation, but she couldn't escape a business built around her personal brand. I asked her, "Would you like to quit your business and go back to being a lawyer?"

She had a momentary flashback of being under strict scrutiny, long hours away from home, and a lucrative yet capped salary, hustling daily in a constrictive suit. With the success of her business, she worked from home and did what she really loved while being dressed in casual outfits that aligned with her free spirit, while she made her own hours. She immediately changed her attitude. Choosing the right words changed her attitude, and her social media work had better results for building her reputation and client attraction. She approached her work with more joy.

I encouraged her to address this positive outcome as a confirmation that she is choosing the right thoughts and the right pathway to become the best in her industry. She can learn to love social media, as this is part of the package that comes with her business. Not only that, it's a privilege to be in her position, where $40,000/month is a "meh" month for her, which is an income that most lawyers don't get to earn.

I applied the same principles of choosing the right words to achieve my own milestones, from quitting my day job many years ago and making six figures in my business in the same year.

When it got hard many times in my journey as an author, entrepreneur, and mother juggling my family, managing my clients, and growing my business, I chose new words that powered me up. Instead of "This is so hard," or "Why isn't it working immediately?" I chose, "I'm so privileged to have an online business that supports my family, a free schedule where I can be available for my children, and a personal brand with an audience that loves my work and waits for me to post, so I'm grateful to have these challenges for further growth."

Choosing the right words is how you recondition your mind to make success your habit.

It is important to note that there is no way to recondition your mind by only thinking. You need to reinforce those thoughts with congruent actions, and with repetition, you create habits.

Words create your perspective, which propels your actions.

Actions, with repetition, become your habits. Over time, they become your personality, which continues to shape your consequences, which creates your reality.

Over time, the words you choose become your fate.

CHAPTER FIVE

Competence

Every Bad Bitch's entry requirement.

The Bad Bitch has a quiet confidence born from years of building her competence and knowing her value.

While she works in silence, she celebrates her progress, and the results speak to impress.

Competence is:

- Proficiency in a specific skill that you're naturally talented at.

- Practicing this skill puts you in the flow, excites you, and makes a contribution to others.

- Therefore, this skill makes you money while you make a difference.

The Bad Bitch already figured out what her strength is and doubled down on polishing it to become highly proficient.

Her goal is to eventually reach Mastery of this skill and become one of the best in the world.

Her strength is the source of her ambition.

Helping others with it is her purpose.

Making a difference with it is her legacy.

The ambition and her strength have a reciprocal effect that expands one another.

The more the Bad Bitch works on her ambition, the more her competence increases.

The more she becomes competent, the more ambitiously driven she becomes to achieve more.

The higher she reaches for, the more competence is required, and the more she dedicates herself to her craft.

Ambition and competence have a positive, reciprocal relationship.

The default state for the Good Girl is *confusion*.

She is an indecisive floater because she's self-unaware.

She thinks that she's multi-passionate, multi-talented, and a Renaissance woman like da Vinci.

You are lost because you can't tell the difference between your strengths and weaknesses.

Instead of finding your strength, you spend a lot of time asking, "Will this work make me money?"

You keep waiting to find out what's realistic for you.

You disregard your talent and your ambition because you think it's unrealistic to make a living with it.

This isn't your fault.

You were conditioned to fail because you were taught to ignore your strengths while spending many years being encouraged to improve your weaknesses.

Your childhood went like this.

Let's say that you find out you're musically gifted, but you struggle in mathematics.

Along with your family and teacher's urging, you spend five days a week studying math and maybe an hour a week playing the piano as a reward for practicing your math.

This is how everyone in society is misguided to take a path of unhappiness and mediocrity; spending minimum time on your strength and spending most of your life trying to make your weakness a strength.

It just doesn't work.

After a childhood of working on your weaknesses, your environment directed you to choose a predictable pathway, such as a doctor, engineer, accountant, or lawyer.

Many artists go into the sciences thinking that they need to develop their scientific thinking to become "smarter" and have to retrain their minds, believing that as an artist they won't make any money.

On the other hand, talented potential scientists lack self-belief and settle in menial jobs.

Many talented Good Girls whose spirits have been crushed in their childhood settle for jobs that keep them small, such as entry-level work, administration, or basic sales because they don't know what else to do. They have false beliefs about themselves. They don't know what they're good at.

Now, there's nothing intrinsically wrong with these jobs. All jobs are commendable unless you're going against yourself and killing your own ambition.

You can actually have a "good degree" and a "good job" while still settling for something that makes you unhappy and unfulfilled.

Everyone has something. Every single person was given a gift, but you were never directed to help find yours.

Finding your strength starts with looking at your early life desires and the times you got positive feedback from people for a specific skill.

If you don't know what that is, you have to make the time to honestly assess yourself and consider getting help from someone experienced to help you with this process. Your own biases and false ingrained beliefs about yourself get in the way of seeing the truth. Your family also often carries biased beliefs about you, so you need a third-party expert who can assess you fairly.

Finding your strength requires honesty.

No matter how much you love singing, you can't become a Whitney Houston unless you have a natural talent that you can build on with a lot of practice.

However, a talented singer the likes of Whitney Houston can live her life as an unhappy accountant if she doesn't believe that she can make a living as a singer and doesn't invest her time, energy, and money into the practice.

Having potential isn't a guarantee for your success.

Finding your strength requires you to be honest with yourself, and then building competence requires discipline.

You know what your strength is, but you feel down: "My strength isn't realistic to make a living."

It's not true that artists, writers, performers, influencers, or entrepreneurs don't make money. Plenty do. Many who do aren't world famous. They work their passion, get paid well, and enjoy a beautiful, private life. Those who want fame work for it.

If you don't know them in your current circle, it feels like a pipe dream.

To become competent in your strength, you have to let go of your mental judgments and limitations.

You have to allow yourself to be honest with yourself and look for the smallest clues that give you the truth.

These clues are always there in your childhood.

The most unexpected skillset that calls for the most uncertain pathway will give you the income, happiness, fulfillment, lifestyle, and success that you always dreamed of.

How I Found My Strength

I spent many years as a floating Good Girl.

I had no examples of successful and independent women whom I could consider a mentor figure.

I had no support and was discouraged from finding my strengths. I had to listen to the rules and follow them without any explanation.

Even though I got good grades, I was always reminded of how much better I could do, and most of the focus went on the subjects that I had difficulty with.

By the time I was 12, our family's immigration and life circumstances demanded that I be fluent in three completely different languages: Korean, Spanish, then English.

My father had an international import-export business, and we moved every 5 years. I was born in Seoul, and at age 5, we moved to Buenos Aires, then after going back to Korea when I was 10, at age 11, we moved to Vancouver.

This meant that every five years, I had to adapt to excel in school in a brand-new language.

The natural struggle that came with the challenge of doing school while learning a new language was written off as being unintelligent and incompetent.

It was atypical in my childhood to get any compliments, but something strange happened.

When I was 16, I wrote my dad an email. He had moved back to Korea while going through a midlife crisis, but the move wasn't helping him.

I wrote something that I can't remember, but it was a relatively short email that gave him some kind of insight and hope.

He wrote back within minutes. Inside, it was a note that read something along the lines of, "Your words moved me."

It was so unexpected that I felt dysregulated from this experience.

I couldn't even get up and walk over to the kitchen to get water.

"Did my dad just give me approval?"

My dad had the appearance of Jackie Chan but possessed the demeanor of Donald Trump. He exuded charisma, humor, and an undeniable air of dominance. One of his unique talents was identifying people's vulnerabilities upon first meeting them, and he skillfully exploited these weaknesses to psychologically subdue them. He had a knack for assigning cruel yet strangely fitting nicknames to everyone in our social circle, all based on their particular insecurities.

He certainly never complimented people.

No efforts were ever good enough for him.

All my life, I tried so hard to impress him with my creative artwork, performance, endless hula hooping, cartwheeling, and dancing, and all of those efforts were met with, "Meh."

After reading that email, I sat in my seat for possibly a whole hour.

I didn't know what to do with that information.

I didn't know if it was luck, he was drunk, or if this compliment was genuine.

I had no idea back then that I needed to gather more data on how I could turn this strength with words into a career.

Many years went by, and I spent all of my 20s rebelling against my rigid and oppressive upbringing.

After almost 15 working years trying to succeed as a dancer and a performer, then going into sales and marketing, I still found myself unhappy and unfulfilled. I was a Good Girl floater.

However, I noticed a pattern.

Every time I had success in the workplace, it had to do with the same skill: it was my persuasive, inspiring, and healing words that gave people a vision, which led to high sales and led me to fast promotions.

While I was giving some customers an amazing sales experience through the use of my words, they saw something in me and recruited me to take the next career step.

I interviewed well and got my dream job as I climbed my career ladder every two years.

There were times that I got jobs that I lacked qualifications for because I was able to articulate my transferable skills so well.

Every time I reflected on my career milestones, the same memory of my dad's comment on that Windows 98 computer screen kept haunting me: "Your words moved me."

Maybe this was also why I got a university degree in literature, even though I thought that I had made a random choice on my part because I was so confused and didn't know what major to pick. I was convinced that I got a useless degree. It wasn't career-directed, and it didn't help me get a job after graduation.

At 22, I entered the job force and could only find the most basic entry-level jobs without much room for growth. I thought I didn't have any money skills.

After floating for 11 years since university graduation, at 33, I realized that I had to hone the strength I have with people and words.

I had to somehow make this my career.

Suddenly, my university degree wasn't useless. All the detours I had in my career made sense.

Once I acknowledged my strength, the confusion cleared, and all of my life's puzzles seemed to resolve before my eyes.

I had to become competent in this skill and get paid for it.

I felt that I had no other choice but to lean in.

I had to be disciplined and recommit to doing my life's work every day.

I saw that this would be the key to becoming happy, wealthy, and fulfilled.

I was full of fear, but I got started.

The results shocked me.

People around me wanted to pay me to coach them.

I naturally excelled, but also had to face the challenges of learning advanced people skills.

I took training on copywriting and human power dynamics, and more than anything, working with so many clients sharpened my competency.

I wrote my first book, and people loved it.

As a coach, author, and social media influencer, everything I do now is, in essence, only an extension of that exact email I wrote my dad when I was 16 years old.

Anytime someone tells me that I've helped them, changed their lives, and sometimes, clients, even social media audiences have written to me, "You've saved me," I feel the same exact overflowing emotions I felt in 1999, frozen, staring at my dad's "Your words moved me."

Even after hundreds of clients, I feel this even now.

CHAPTER SIX

Social Elegance

Elegant people skills become your golden ticket.

The Bad Bitch is a master of human behavior, motivation, and emotions.

She understands human power dynamics and knows how to navigate them to get what she wants.

She has social elegance.

Her success isn't just due to her competence.

She's a master in soft skills.

People love the experience they have with the Bad Bitch, so they collaborate and open doors for her.

That's how she achieves great heights.

The Good Girl has only two tools in her people skills:

The first is to please. She changes, shapeshifts, and conceals her true feelings to give people what they want.

The second is bravado. Her insecurity triggers her to shout, talk big, and fight with people to mask her pent-up sadness, anger, and jealousy, all stemming from a deep-seated sense of inadequacy.

This is why you oscillate between being a nice pleaser and a mean girl.

You're an emotional landmine, easily triggered by small things.

You don't have control over yourself because you are reactive.

That's why you run hot and cold with people.

You manipulate, instead of communicating, because you were never taught *how* to be honest.

This is why your life is so erratic and messy.

The Good Girl thinks she's really good with people as a pleaser, but in reality, she struggles the most in human relationships.

It's common for the Good Girl to surround herself with those much less accomplished than her because they don't threaten her ego.

Her circle comprises toxic people, opportunistic users, and those with low self-awareness, self-esteem, and few boundaries.

She has to be the biggest fish in a small pond.

You choose a partner who may not have a chance to leave you for someone better. You count on their brokenness, disconnection, insecurity, and even unattractiveness to appease your fear of abandonment. You fight to feel safe. You have to feel like they can never leave you.

Your friendship group reflects the same.

You're either a loner, or you friend down, surrounding yourself with less accomplished, struggling individuals who won't challenge you. You share with them an invisible connection with the same fears around human relationships and the inability to face conflict.

When you meet accomplished people, you feel intimidated, small, judged, criticized, and overwhelmed.

Honesty, no matter how well-worded, feels like a slap in the face. Helpfulness and care feel like pity, and you really don't want that.

You want to be influenced by impressionable people, but you feel too triggered by their presence.

When you live on autopilot, pleasing and serving those around you, you desensitize from your emotions to cope. Certain successful people awaken your desensitized fear to the surface. It's overwhelming.

You pull away.

The cycle continues.

When you don't feel safe, you keep giving undeserving people your energy to "fix it," to feel safe.

You can't receive.

Your confusion, indecision, and shapeshifting are frustrating to people who expect professionalism, clear communication, and reciprocity.

Toxic people gather around you because they know that feeding you with a bit of validation will boost your ego, and you'll voluntarily be open to being used to fulfill their desires.

People with boundaries and leadership feel unfamiliar to you, so you misinterpret them as disliking you, being cold, or even using you.

The Good Girl has undeveloped social skills, and therefore she doesn't understand people at all. She doesn't understand how the world actually works. Even when she's proven wrong, she argues that her views are right. She's always the victim of some narcissist or someone jealous, not realizing how she contributed to the problem with her own behaviors.

Guilt, shame, and blame are the Good Girl's excuses.

Your lens is contaminated by the abusive power dynamics and poor leadership you experienced in childhood.

You push well-meaning people away.

Even when you want a better life, to be loved, admired, and nurtured, you can't help but to choose the familiar toxic patterns in relationships. To cope, you keep reacting in that environment the same way you always did in your family.

You call this your "reality" and your "personality."

People with good intentions don't feel safe around you. They know something is "off" about you. They may never tell you because they don't want to deal with your reactions, but it's true.

You don't know how to give and receive value with successful people who have the capacity to make your life better. You're polite, but you don't know how to respect people because you weren't respected.

You don't know how to cope with stress without self-sabotaging with binging, drinking, shopping, or taking it out on others.

You don't know how to handle conflict without avoiding the issue all together, pretending like nothing happened, or becoming righteous and adversarial towards others.

You're not self-aware enough. You don't realize that you behave exactly the way the adults did in your childhood home and exactly like those who once hurt you through their unconscious, self-unaware behaviors.

Even though you decided to be better than those who hurt you, these patterns are deeply ingrained in you, and you automatically play them out in relationships.

This is why your life never seems to get better.

If you ever tell the Good Girl that she isn't good with people, she'll take it as the greatest insult and be very offended.

You're likely offended now, but if you want to change, you need to overcome this trigger and stay with me to become the Bad Bitch you're meant to be.

The Bad Bitch is nuanced.

She is great with people. She doesn't try to please or manipulate them.

She has an array of sophisticated weapons. She's strategic.

Her social elegance is more than basic etiquette or pleasantness.

She can read a person quickly, and within a few minutes, she understands what they may be lacking or needing.

From this point, she'll assess how this person can fit into her journey of reaching her ambition.

Before you get confused, the Bad Bitch is not a user.

She knows that quality reciprocity creates a centrifugal force that lifts each other into an upward spiral of success.

She is fair.

She understands that in the long run, how someone remembers her interaction matters more than what she can get from that person in that moment.

She cares while always looking after herself.

She always approaches relationships with curiosity and with the desire to add value, while considering how she and the other person could have a win-win situation together.

The Bad Bitch is secure, and therefore, she knows that the only way to get ahead is to associate with those who are committed, accomplished, and successful.

Her company is vibrant mix of significant, successful, and very interesting people.

She is a small fish in a big ocean, striving to expand and grow to match the size of the vastness.

She knows that embodying excellent people skills always has room for improvement, and therefore she makes it a priority to be better at it.

Empathy development is the foundation of social elegance.

The Bad Bitch can come across as intimidating because she doesn't manipulate to communicate. While being direct and honest, she considers her words carefully to make sure that they land well with the other person. She is respectful.

Once you're in her presence and open yourself up, she's the most generous, giving, and nurturing person you will ever meet.

She's emotionally intelligent and therefore has an incredible capacity to hold space for people.

She foresees your behavior before you even know you are going to do it.

The Bad Bitch and her social elegance is a rare beauty that you'll experience.

Not many people have her emotional intelligence, compassion, and depth of empathy.

She understands different industries, cultures, and history.

She is educated in social justice issues and marginalized group experiences, even when these issues don't apply to her.

To become the Bad Bitch, the Good Girl needs to expand her empathy.

You talk about being an empath all the time, but you actually have very limited and selective empathy.

You are stunted because you were never taught how to respond instead of reacting.

You get triggered, judge, and jump to conclusions too fast.

You blame.

You become the victim.

Your paranoia from intense fears creates resistance to trust, which means that there can't be any communication.

Instead of inquiring, you accuse.

Instead of giving people power, you try to save them.

When you don't get it, you immediately rule out unfamiliar concepts and beliefs as wrong.

People don't feel inspired around you. Even when you think you're caring about others, you're being self-involved. Others feel judged and dismissed.

When it's outside of your lived experience, you're unable to show support or even open your mind to understand what someone's emotional experience could be to bear that type of challenge. This is a sign of limited empathy.

When you're emotionally blocked, you can't access empathy, and without empathy, you can't understand human experiences. You can't understand people, which means you lack people skills.

You also can't be wise. Wisdom is a combination of skills, experience, and emotional intelligence.

Your emotional block doesn't allow you to genuinely connect with others. You overshare to attempt to break down this wall, but it makes it worse.

When you witness someone's struggle, you quickly make it about yourself, speaking of your own experience, and how you feel.

When oversharing creates more of a divide, you believe that it's your trauma experiences that make you so unique, special, and different. You think that others are not sophisticated enough to understand you.

You unwittingly create greater walls between you and others.

You feel that nobody can understand you because you're so amazing and unique, not realizing that this is a projection that you don't understand others.

You falsely believe that being a pleaser and crying with someone about injustice is being empathetic.

You falsely interpret empathy to mean you have to give up your boundaries and submit to others. Not only do you allow this, but you also do it to others, as this is your expectation.

You accidentally exhibit ignorance and breach people's boundaries by righteously pushing your ignorance onto them.

When you're naïve, you mean well, but you do harm.

The Bad Bitch is a master at managing relationships.

She's aware of her emotions and triggers.

Her empathy spectrum is vast and wide.

This is why she can read people so well and just *gets* people.

She notices people's facial and body expressions to tap into hidden, suppressed emotions.

She understands people from all walks of life without ever having experienced her struggles.

From there, she finds out what people may need from her.

When you meet her and have a conversation with her, you'll feel addicted to her energy.

In an unempathetic world, once you have a dose of the Bad Bitch, she feels like an oasis in the midst of a desert.

That's because she read you and gave you exactly what you needed.

Embodying social elegance is the most essential skill development for your success because when you leave a remarkably positive impression on people, they hand you the golden ticket, which creates doors where there were no doors. They build bridges for you. They lend you a ladder so you easily level up.

This embodiment is *executive presence*.

The Bad Bitch is a leader.

No matter where you find her in her life, you'll eventually see that she rises to the top of her industry.

She carries herself well.

She's likable and trustworthy because she's warm and competent.

She commands respect through her actions and words.

She is a clear communicator.

When speaking her true thoughts, she goes straight to the point, while elegantly smoothing out the edges to make sure the words land softly.

She is concise and succinct.

She makes people's lives simple.

She makes hard work feel less burdensome.

This is why she leaves a fine impression on people.

The Bad Bitch is secure, elegant, eloquent, and sophisticated, which means she can carry interesting conversations and build relationships with people who are more successful than her, even with those who are completely far out from her own life and work experiences.

She surrounds herself with competent, socially elegant leaders from her industry.

If the Bad Bitch was a book, she'd be *How to Win Friends and Influence People*.

It isn't unheard of that a company will make a special position only for her, or a director will write a movie part just based on her, and people will come back to her years later and appreciate her for something she said to them many years back that helped them.

People call her lucky, but luck has a formula.

Social elegance is how the Bad Bitch becomes self-made.

How to develop social elegance:

1. Learn to **listen** without speaking and needing to be the center of attention.

2. **Educate** yourself in philosophy, cultures, and experiences that are far from yours.

3. Gather **sophisticated friendships** from all different types of backgrounds, and practice listening to their perspectives and experiences.

4. Ask them for their **perspective** on your ideas and thoughts, and reflect on how you come across to others.

5. Before you jump to conclusions, ask "Why?" with **curiosity**.

6. Be **respectful**. No matter how well you know someone, don't become lazy and blurt words out. Think and feel the words before you say them. Make sure that the words land softly to bypass defensiveness. Only then can communication take place.

This Bad Bitch's Social Elegance Doubled Her Salary

Francesca Valentina found me via some LinkedIn posts and articles I had written. She was a leader in the not-for-profit sector and was in between jobs. She was about to start a COO position, which she began shortly after we started working together.

In her past managerial positions, she had a pattern of overextending herself, overworking, and trying to nurture everyone until she crumbled. Many of her past bosses told her to work on her executive presence.

She understood that her challenge was rooted in experiencing extreme adversity in her upbringing. She was a foster child who aged out of the system. As a child, she experienced a lot of physical, sexual, and drug abuse. She never experienced a stable home life with mature parental figures, which meant that she never had the chance to learn social elegance. She only observed unhealthy reactions to conflict and behavioral examples of what not to do. Even though she did her best to be better, willpower and intentions alone couldn't undo the effects of childhood.

Francesca had a naturally healing soul. She was driven by advocacy and was determined to make a difference in people's lives. She had the best intentions, yet every time she faced challenging interpersonal conflicts, her reactive coping mechanisms got in the way.

Like most people, Francesca thought that her workplace was going to teach her how to navigate the power dynamics at work. Over time, she learned that work cultures do not have the resources nor the capabilities to extend soft skills training to their employees.

Francesca did her best. She did years of therapy and attended leadership retreats, yet she ran into the same interpersonal stresses in multiple workplaces. She repeated the patterns of coping until she burned out and crumbled. She always got similar feedback from her supervisors to improve her executive presence, but they did not give her anything more to help her.

Francesca became aware that she had to find another way to change. Her coping mechanisms were getting in the way of her promotions. She relied on her work ethic to overcome her shortcomings in executive presence. Once she got to a C-level position, her hard work couldn't mask her social elegance challenges.

As a new COO, Francesca had no issue with the hard skills. She was effective, productive, and got the job done well. Her leadership skills when managing 75 subordinates became the stubborn glass ceiling. She was struggling with pressure from upper management while overextending to save her subordinates from a toxic culture. The stress started to take a toll on her mental and physical health to the point that she needed to quit the job.

She knew this wasn't what she wanted.

We worked on turning the reactiveness into socially elegant responsiveness. She needed to feel safe in her body, which was far from familiar for her. Once she embodied safety, she had a much better vision of what she wanted in her career. Her energy became open to opportunities. She felt good about herself, which meant that she became open to connecting with others. She networked consistently and spoke to many leaders in the not-for-profit sector who were impressed by her remarkable story of survival, combined with experience, knowledge, and work ethic.

She was offered an Executive Director position that supported foster youth development, which aligned much better with Francesca's life purpose than the COO position she was in.

In her upgrading process, she doubled her salary while, for the first time, experiencing true happiness and alignment.

Opportunities didn't stop there.

She was nominated and was chosen as a Fellow along with many national leaders in the National Leadership Circle with Foster America.

Francesca went from being a Good Girl to a Bad Bitch by becoming aware of her triggers, learning to regulate her emotions, and becoming responsive, not reactive.

CHAPTER SEVEN

Non-Committal

When you say "Yes" to priorities, you're saying "No" to the rest.

The Good Girl commits quickly, to everything and everyone.

She commits to what sabotages her.

She is loyal to her workplace even if they pay her shit and treat her badly, and even when she doesn't get the promotion that she deserves.

She's loyal to her family and the people who hurt her even when they don't see her value and continue to treat her like she's inferior.

She calls it diplomatic when she's nice to these people who don't see her for who she really is and her capabilities.

As the Good Girl, you commit to the wrong things.

Many years ago, I worked with a woman named Dorothy.

She was so addicted to cigarettes that she couldn't go without multiple smoke breaks.

This was a problem in a sales job where she earned a commission, as the amount on her paycheck depended on her being present.

One day, I couldn't hold back.

Dorothy was so good at her job, and I couldn't stand her leaving again to smoke when she could be making bank.

She might as well light up $100 bills and smoke that!

"Dorothy, why don't you quit smoking? Look at how much it's damaging your health and your bank account!"

"Julia, I'm not a quitter!"

She flashed me the biggest smile and left to join the backdoor addiction gang, who all seemed to understand each other through the rhythmic sucking and puffing, without sharing any words.

Dorothy was charming, but she was also wrong.

She was a quitter.

She quit on her financial and physical health.

She was using cigarettes as a vice to avoid her inner demons, so she was quitting on her mental health.

The Good Girl is tenacious with what harms her while effortlessly quitting on what's good for her.

I quit that sales job to do something bigger with myself. I had bigger goals. I knew that job was a temporary stepping stone for me.

It was a place where I was learning persuasion and influence, every single day. Nine months in this job was enough for me.

I never settled in a job for longer than two years. I was always looking for new ways to ladder up to the next level.

I knew that I had to be an opportunistic climber to move up in my career ladder based on the skills I needed next to become a successful entrepreneur and coach.

I went from sales to financial services to working in a tech corporate environment. During these two positions, I was already side-hustling in coaching. As my next move, I quit and went all-in with my business.

All of the skills and experiences I gathered from those career moves became the foundation of my coaching. Nothing was wasted.

Dorothy was a Good Girl. She was just as smart as I was, but she didn't believe in herself, nor even have an idea about what her ambitions were. So she stayed working in commission retail.

Good Girls have dreams. They are smart. They contemplate. But they don't bet on themselves, instead, they bet on their vices.

Addiction guarantees that you'll feel good in that moment, but it keeps you where you are.

You are a short-term player because that's what we as humans do when we're living in survival mode, which is living in fear. When you're afraid, you can't quit on what gives you short-term pleasure and even a false sense of safety.

But in that process, you quit on yourself.

You commit to temporary solutions and forget your true potential.

The Bad Bitch has only one commitment: Her legacy.

She has a long-term vision. She knows how she wants to be known, what difference she'll make with her work, and how she wants to raise her heirs, if she has any.

Her commitment in a sentence is what an old Korean proverb states: "A tiger leaves its skin after its death, and a [wo]man leaves [her] name after [her] death."

She picks and chooses what aligns with her own first and only commitment.

She doesn't commit to any job, a man, friends, or even her own family if they get in the way of the commitment to her legacy.

To the Good Girl, the Bad Bitch is cold, ruthless, and has harsh boundaries.

However, the Bad Bitch is fair.

She values reciprocity.

She values growth over making a commitment.

Commitment to a man, a job, or any obligations, compete with your focus on your ambition.

The Bad Bitch is wise. She eliminates obstacles to make her success process to keep it as simple as possible.

To do that, she assesses and removes complications.

That's why she only commits to herself, her purpose, and her legacy.

This approach does everyone around her a favor.

She allows people to take responsibility for their own growth. She doesn't try to control or save anyone who can't meet her where she is.

She promptly releases and lets go of outdated opportunities.

She evaluates even blood family and old friends to assess them: are they capable of adding value to her life, or do their limitations and judgments act as an obstacle?

She is honest.

She releases relationships when reciprocity isn't possible anymore.

A workplace is more than a salary. It's a place to polish her strengths and competence and to expand her mind. Once she learns what she needs to learn, she will move up and on.

The Bad Bitch is non-committal.

That's why when you find a happy Bad Bitch, you often find her single and loving it, building her empire.

WHEN I GAVE BACK THE DIAMOND, MY LIFE BEGAN

When I look back on my purposeful journey, finding my strength, believing in it, and overcoming my own fears to bet on myself, there was a catalytic moment of no return.

The life I have now wouldn't be possible if I didn't give back that diamond and platinum ring so many years ago.

In my early 30s, I was a single mom with two young children, and finances were tough.

My whole circle at the time comprised people who were brainwashed by patriarchy and wanted to see me paired up again as quickly as possible.

They were either single moms looking to find a new guy to rely on, singles who were looking for commitment, or married people living in the illusion of happiness, who felt the need to defend their life choices by forcing them on others.

When I started dating this man three years into single motherhood, it was due to three reasons:

1. It was a rebound from my separation, an 8-year relationship that gave me two children.

2. Life was so tough that I needed an escape, in a typical Good Girl fashion.

3. I was being mentally pulled by the toxic patriarchal group-think environment that a woman's ultimate happiness is to be paired up with a man.

After seven months of dating, it was Valentine's Day. He gave me a diamond and platinum ring.

My first gut instinct was very uncomfortable. I already saw in our previous interactions that there was a lot more that needed to be figured out before commitment could even be considered.

I was in a career transition, and he was too.

When differences in value systems came up in a conversation, such as social justice issues, I noticed that he wanted to avoid and change the topic. He didn't like honest conversations.

However, he came around wanting to help all the time, taking care of the little things to free up my time and energy. Those efforts pulled the relationship forward.

Although he was careful to hide some of his true thoughts by not speaking much, through his words, I noticed deep ignorance, a lot of unresolved trauma, a lack of social awareness, and entitlement that comes from ignorance.

I was investing in myself to grow my mindset, and I didn't see any evidence of him doing the same. He wasn't someone to voluntarily pay a coach or a therapist to work on himself.

I had been engaged and investing in my own self-development for years, and I was willing to do a lot more.

Even with all this context, when I told my whole circle that he gave me a diamond ring, they were all happy for me.

The same people were not happy when I became single, even when I did the right thing for myself and my children. They judged or pitied me. The same people also judged me and talked negatively whenever I was leaving my job for the next upgrade or when I later started my own business.

Essentially, whenever I spoke or acted non-committal, my circle questioned me, sometimes ignoring me for months, giving me clear signs that there was something wrong with me, as I made them uncomfortable.

The Good Girl caves under this type of peer pressure. She feels guilty. She feels shame. In this scenario, she blames herself. She feels bad about disappointing people who will never have to bear the consequences of her life decisions, even after pressuring her to take a sabotaging road. She shapeshifts and betrays herself.

The Bad Bitch endures.

I knew that accepting this ring meant that I would have to carry the burden of this commitment with me, and that burden was a man who wasn't capable of working on his own mindset and growth.

After a few days of thinking, I gave him back the ring.

That must have triggered his ego badly from rejection because he almost immediately broke up with me.

That non-committal move was a Bad Bitch move that propelled me to bet on myself even more.

It felt bad initially, but it gave me a huge boost in confidence to do the right thing for myself, which gave me the confirmation that remaining non-committal was the elevating pathway.

In the following 18 months to come, I took the greatest personal and career risks, jumping into a new job every nine months to elevate my skills, until I confidently started my own coaching business.

Consequently, my income almost tripled, and I was doing work that mattered the most to me.

After five years of steady success, my assistant informed me of a strange email.

It was that same man trying to get through to me via my business email, asking how things were.

I went and Googled him. He had started his own business. I read the Google reviews left for his business.

There were many good reviews, but also many reviews reported negative experiences from his customers addressing unhinged behavior, which clearly stemmed from mindset problems.

I had a slight moment of thought of where my life would be if I had decided to take on the burden of that diamond ring. I'm certain that I'd be nowhere near where I am now.

My life would have been like a three-legged race, where I would have to keep encouraging him to painstakingly move forward, while sabotaging the speed of my own success, trying to carry his unhealed and irresponsible burden to move forward.

Worse, I couldn't imagine where my children would be in that mess because they are the only ones that deserve to be considered on my success journey, as they are a part of my legacy.

Remaining non-committal to people's opinions, a job, any boss or colleague that you like, even a long-term friend, blood family, or a man, allows you to fly at high speed to reach your desires.

Chapter Eight

Unbothered

Success doesn't care about your feelings.

N
o matter what you're trying to achieve, your greatest obstacles will always be people.

No matter how much you want to stay non-committal, people will pressure you to commit and please.

When you look after your own interests, you inevitably make people uncomfortable.

When a woman fights for her ambition, people's misogynistic unconscious bias programming reflects back to them. "Who does she think she is?"

Envy is the most common human emotion.

Inevitably, many, even those closest to her who smile at her daily, secretly want to see her taken down.

Observe any siblings, friendship groups, or any space where humans congregate, and you'll inevitably see competition and power struggles.

Competition and rivalry stem from envy.

Under patriarchy, women are programmed to compete. The Good Girl has to compete to be chosen, to be patriarchy's teacher's pet, and to be better than other women to survive. From the moment girls have interactions with their peers, they play the "I'm better than you" game.

Girls become women, and they don't grow out of it. Most women in our society are Good Girls. We are raised to be, and most stay this way. Toxic patriarchal competition rules grown women's lives and careers. Housewives, and corporate and businesswomen alike tirelessly compete with other women, running a never-ending comparison list in their minds against other women they know, about who is the most stylish, prettiest, richest, smartest, and socially advantaged.

Women falsely believe that when they leave an all-women environment, the stressful competition will stop. This isn't true at all. The competition thickens in male-dominated industries where there are fewer women and the number of seats for women is visibly scarce.

The Good Girl gets swept up and swallowed in the mess. The Bad Bitch learns to surpass and move up and on.

The Good Girl becomes the Bad Bitch as she painstakingly learns the laws of power and embodies them in her conduct and strategic planning on how to deal with people around her.

No matter how much humans have the intention to create equality in a group, equality isn't possible, because naturally, humans want hierarchy, and a hierarchical power structure will form.

The Good Girl wants to stay blind to all this.

Your mind is frozen from years of oppression, and your way to cope is to see the world in a more "positive" way.

Then, when you get fed up, you yell, fight, and act in bravado, thinking that this is power. This isn't. It's anti-power.

You're triggered, which weakens your position even further, creating further damage to those you want to care for and protect.

What you don't process becomes your weakness.

Your whole life is a curated charade to avoid setting off your triggers. You can't honestly admit your weaknesses. You pretend to not have any, when you have plenty, and other people can see them and use them against you. You can't look at your own pain, and therefore, you can't heal what really needs to be healed.

The Bad Bitch spends a lot of time looking at those areas.

That's how she built her mindset to become resilient.

She invested a lot in healing and processing her hidden triggers.

She had many difficult instances where she had to bet on herself.

This is how she became so self-aware, which is the first and most important step to understanding people.

That's why no matter what kind of industry she is in, the Bad Bitch is an expert in human psychology.

She understands why people do the things that they do and why they don't.

She understands that very few people actually want to see her succeed and the majority of the people want to see her fail.

This is the opposite of the Good Girl who thinks that most people want to see her succeed, which is absolutely not true.

That's how you get screwed over.

That's how you get betrayed.

That's how you get blindsided.

This doesn't happen to the Bad Bitch for a very simple reason; the Bad Bitch knows how people and the world work.

The Good Girl is naïve.

She sees people and the world how she wishes they were.

Her magic thinking and rose-colored glasses are trauma responses to conceal what hurts while they keep harming her, but she thinks that this mindset makes her a positive person. As if proving how much she suffers "earns" her a reward later.

This is how the Good Girl gets blindsided, when the Bad Bitch already saw it coming.

The Bad Bitch is experienced and, therefore, understands that people are risk factors.

She's aware that everyone is performing, and it's up to her to see people below the surface of who they really are.

That's why a Bad Bitch is never shocked or victimized when people turn on her, betray her, run hot and cold, or even attempt to sabotage her by smearing her reputation.

She reads people's behavioral patterns and does damage control ahead of time because she actually expects this kind of behavior from most people.

Doing so, she protects herself. She doesn't get involved and become influenced by other people's agenda to take someone down via highly convincing gossip. She understands that most are deeply insecure and self-unaware, and talking behind someone's back always has a hidden agenda that serves the gossiper.

She is aware that our minds get influenced easily even when we don't want to be influenced, and therefore, she keeps her circle clean by removing people who exhibit frequent toxic behaviors. She understands that gossipers cause harm even when the gossip initially doesn't involve her. They will later do the same to her, or they may harm her by influencing her to lose trust in someone who truly has her back. Allying with people with toxic behaviors always weakens her position, which creates lasting detriment.

She understands that people project their insecurities onto a person. This is why haters act out, attempt to smear your reputation, and manipulate other people to hate you.

When facing the counterforces, the Good Girl gets consumed in negativity for a long time. She may recover to some level, but ruminations for years to come get the best of her. She may even quit.

The Bad Bitch still feels.

Even when she foresees problems coming, she feels hurt because as non-committal as she is, she still cares greatly about relationships.

The Bad Bitch remains resilient by processing and learning from the relationships and returns to unbotheredness really quickly.

That's why she's unstoppable.

THIS BAD BITCH MADE BILLIONS OUT OF GOSSIP AND BETRAYAL

While every public figure, celebrity, and even micro-influencer has to master the art of unbotheredness, many, if not most, drown and dissipate under the negativity black hole.

Taylor Swift is an artist whose specialty was built around alchemizing envy, betrayal, and gossip to turn them into billions over the course of her career.

You can love her or hate her, but Taylor does this one thing really well: alchemizing hate into profit.

Her catchy songs depict stories of lovers who take her for a ride and even female friends who betrayed her.

She made a lucrative singer-songwriter career out of negative gossip and attempted character assassination from various counterforces who were deeply triggered by a young woman reaching world-class success in her ambition.

Her early songs were all about heartbreaks from men who didn't see her value. This was her initial claim to fame, which became more pronounced as she progressed in her career.

It was 2009, and she was 20 years old and a rookie when she was receiving the Video Music Award. In her moment of glory, an accomplished male musician, who was much older than her, went up on the stage to steal her thunder. He announced to the world on that stage that she didn't deserve that award, but Beyoncé did.

This moment's snapshot went viral on the internet, which isn't how an artist wants to go viral, but Taylor used that opportunity to respond with great social elegance.

It boosted her profile and made her a true household name. Her fans later speculated that the music in the album *reputation* was about this incident, which raked in over a million dollars in sales during the first week, being one of the best-selling albums in 2017.

Her fans became obsessed with Taylor's ongoing feud and drama with various celebrities and her way of responding: demonstrating great social elegance in interviews and creating catchy clap backs through her music.

Taylor consistently monetized her struggles in romantic relationships and friendship fallouts. She repeated the same patterns over and over again, where her romantic interests and her girl squad disintegrated before the media's eyes. Almost every Taylor song is about love, a few about friendship fallouts, and many are about media scrutiny. Her song "Shake It Off" from the album *1989* is one of her best-selling songs and is about **being unbothered**.

Taylor demonstrated the exact Bad Bitch unbotheredness formula; her feelings always got hurt, but she quickly recovered by alchemizing the situation by learning from it, and making a ton of money from the experience was always a part of her process.

Another highly publicized betrayal took over the media by storm involving Taylor's former friend and music industry executive, Scooter Braun.

In June 2019, it was announced that Scooter Braun's company, Ithaca Holdings, had acquired the rights to Taylor Swift's entire catalog of master recordings, including her early albums.

This acquisition was particularly distressing for Taylor Swift because she had a long-standing feud with Scooter Braun.

The betrayal felt deeply personal, as she had previously considered him a friend and mentor.

Taylor Swift publicly expressed her frustration and disappointment in the situation, stating that she was never given the opportunity to own her music.

The incident led to a significant dispute and heightened discussions about artists' rights and ownership within the music industry.

In 2021, Taylor made it known to the public that she began to re-record her music to own the rights to them. All her fans redirected their focus to listen to the new versions of her music, called "Taylor's Version." She released some new music along with re-recorded versions of her old music. This process deepened the sympathy and respect towards her from her fans and the public who were adamant about helping her claim justice in an unjust situation.

After gaining the attention and love of her fans through the process of being the beautiful hero in her injustice story, she shortly announced the Eras Tour in 2022, after a tour hiatus since 2018.

Tickets were sold out within minutes of going on sale, estimated to have made $590 million, as many more tour dates were being added.

Taylor's ongoing money machine strategy has a repetitive pattern of fanfare of criticism around her dating life, friendships, and even business deals, which gets her fans invested in her story. Taylor writes songs about it while playing the bigger person.

Her fans are addicted to her unbotheredness because that's a quality that they all wish they had. They are vicariously living boldly through Taylor's music, wanting to become the Bad Bitch by feeling Taylor's energy through her music.

Most people develop a thick skin to attempt to ignore the counterforces so they don't sabotage themselves. They attempt to manage their emotions so they don't get distracted from climbing to succeed.

Taylor's Bad Bitch strategy didn't stop at managing her emotions from negative human experiences. She uses the negativity as ladders to climb higher, build her reputation, and to make more money.

Unbothereness made her rich, and alchemizing criticism into power will make you rich and happy too.

CHAPTER NINE

Audacity

"Fortune favors the bold." - Latin Proverb

The Bad Bitch is audacious in her ambition, and she follows through by taking equally audacious actions.

She doesn't act bold to prove herself. Boldness is a form of her most authentic expression on the pathway of turning her ambition into reality.

Audaciousness is what makes her a magnetic powerhouse.

She shines brightly as the main character.

The Good Girl has big dreams too, but she mostly lives in contemplation.

She stays hidden, where she feels safe from judgment and criticism.

She takes a few actions here and there to appease herself: "I'm doing something!"

She lives so carefully; therefore, she has no personality.

She's boring.

You are controlled by fear. You're performing to be appropriate. That's why boldness is painful for you. That's why you don't stand out. That's why you're "stuck."

Your actions are nowhere near what's required for you to make a stride.

Your mind always says, "What I want is impossible," "I don't want to hurt someone's feelings," "I don't want to be wrong in front of a lot of people."

These words keep you in contemplation, and it's why you stay stagnant, after years and decades.

The Bad Bitch always expands out of her comfort zone. She faces her fears. She takes calculated risks. She bets on herself.

It's what makes her shine.

The Good Girl wants everyone to tell her that she is a star. She spends most of her time talking about what makes her so special and her huge dreams. She doesn't continue to invest enough in the work that will actually help her claim stardom.

Even when she experiences moments of significant success or goes viral, she can't keep up the momentum; she gets swept away by it. In the midst of her addiction to validation, she becomes pompous and loses people's trust.

The Good Girl chases. She's desperate. She's a try-hard. She gets dragged by what she *thinks* will give her the attention, which is almost always wrong.

A star *attracts*.

The Bad Bitch is a star. She makes aligned moves and people follow her.

She doesn't need people to tell her that she's a star because she knows that she is one.

She shines, giving people just enough to keep them excited, then goes back to the drawing board to plan her next moves.

Even though some may suspect that she's full of herself, she isn't. When she's planning her next moves and creating new work, she's always centering on those she's leading, including her subordinates, audience, readers, or viewers.

Even when she doesn't look like she's working, she's learning new skills, networking with the right people, and watching the market.

She works in silence to attract less counterforces. She surprises with actions, which to others, seem crazy, bold, risky, unexpected, and nonsensical.

To the Bad Bitch, all her moves make sense because she decided long ago that she had no other option but to turn her ambition into reality.

While doing what it takes, she keeps her fingers on the pulse of change.

She is keenly aware of social and pop culture trends, as well as the ever-changing consumer behavior. She's ready to jump on trends to give herself a faster boost to success.

For example, if witches and magic are trending, she will create products, such as party decor or clothing, or write a book based on those themes.

If a celebrity or a show is trending, she will use those themes to create social media engagement.

When a new social media platform gains momentum, she's on it, studying it, and testing it out before anyone else in her circle is. This is how social media influencers are born. They are usually the early adopters. You increase your chance to win when you start early.

Watching trends and the market does many things for the Bad Bitch.

It opens up her mind to opportunities because she's an opportunist, in the most respectful way.

When you watch trends, what used to be uncool eventually becomes cool. For example, hip hop was once an underground artform. It started developing in the 1970s by the African-American youth in Bronx, NY, and for a long time, it was given little merit and respect. It started to become mainstream in the '90s and has ruled every aspect of popular trend and style to become a worldwide pop culture standard.

When you wait long enough, your most embarrassing aspects become what makes you magnetic. I was once embarrassed of my South Korean background. Growing up in the West since I was five, I recall the kids at school not even knowing where Korea was on the world map. I always had Korean stationery, fashion, face cream, and as a teen, makeup, and this made me feel different and uncool. In the early 2000s K-drama and K-pop started to become popular globally. More recently, K-beauty started to take off worldwide. Now, every teenager is listening to K-pop and so many are obsessed with K-beauty. Currently, Korean is becoming so mainstream worldwide that it's the next worldwide pop culture standard. Now when I mention that I'm Korean, many people unconsciously categorize me as "cool." Due to the change of trends, suddenly, my once embarrassing origin unexpectedly became a social advantage.

The Bad Bitch keeps up to use anything she can, including unconscious biases of the people and the evolving consumer's mindset, to her advantage.

Even in industries, what used to be looked down upon can suddenly become a respectable, lucrative profession.

In the past, pole dancing was considered the most lowbrow form of dance. Now, pole dancing has been embraced by women who want to own their sensuality as a form of expression. Although it was once considered lowbrow, many conservative, wealthy women take up pole dance to loosen up and feel more free. Pole has become an art form and a fitness sport.

There are pole dance conventions and competitions all over the world. Women invest thousands of dollars to learn and to become proficient at it. Many dance and fitness studios offer pole lessons, and there are even dedicated pole-only studios. It is no longer a lowbrow dance, nor about pleasing the male gaze. It has become a symbol of women taking control and owning their sensuality and authenticity. It's now a lucrative industry, from classes to apparel.

One of my clients, Ariel Xenia, is a social media influencer and a celebrated pole teacher in Nashville. As a former ballet dancer, she now makes a lucrative full-time living as a pole teacher. Even twenty years ago, her career wouldn't have been viable. Ariel has thriving online pole classes, gets invited to different studios to run workshops, and goes to vacation destinations like Bali to teach retreat pole workshops.

The Bad Bitch is always audacious.

She jumps into a line of work or a trend before it becomes cool. She also blends different aspects of her strengths, talents, and magnetism to stand out in an already saturated market.

THIS BAD BITCH MADE A RICH CREATIVE CAREER WITH "MENIAL SKILLS"

As a teen, YouTuber Moriah Elizabeth started out making funny skits, some featuring her younger brother. She had great comedic timing and a charismatic stage presence, but this alone didn't shoot her up to YouTube stardom.

One day, she did something totally different. She posted a video of her making DIY squishies. Her videos were different from other DIY videos because she was funny, as she always had been in all her videos. At the time, squishies were a trending toy. Every kid in elementary school had a few.

Her video started to take off.

Next, she posted a video of her doing a squishy repair. Squishies are a fragile sponge toy that rip easily, which if it happened to a child with their favorite squishy, it would be devastating. Moriah's repair video helped to meet this unseen audience need.

She went viral.

She took her cue from the audience and changed her channel direction. She dedicated it to showcase her arts and crafts talent. The viral squishy videos helped her find her footing. She made her audience a part of her creative process. Viewers could send broken squishies to her P.O. Box so she could fix them on camera.

Her next moves needed to keep her audience wanting more, while monetizing her talents in the arts and crafts business model.

She created really cute characters, gave them quirky names, created some stories around them, and integrated them into her art-making process. She brought her comedic personality into her video editing and narration. Her audience was an engaged community of creatives who loved to be involved. They loved to help Moriah name new characters and help her choose a creative direction for projects.

Her brand became a unique combination of quirky creative process, storytelling, and funny editing. Her outstanding creativity left her viewers addicted for more.

Moriah created an activity book series called *Create This Book*, where people can follow her prompts to unleash their own creativity. She has a thriving e-commerce shop with ongoing, seasonal, and limited edition apparel and merchandise, featuring her cute cartoon creations.

Moriah has a cult following. Every one of her social media accounts shows her followers gushing over and loving every move she makes.

As of now, Moriah's follower count has reached almost 10 million subscribers on YouTube, averaging multi-million views on her videos. She is one of the most successful artist YouTubers.

Most people could not imagine that cartoon drawings that started out as doodles could make someone an estimated millions of dollars.

Moriah observed and went with the flow of her audience's feedback. Her magnetic main character energy is a combination of her creativity, comedic timing, and funny video edits.

There hadn't been any public figure who Moriah could exactly model after. How she showcases her talent is bold. That makes her unique and unforgettable. She is a personality. She is a star.

In this world, there are plenty of creatives who can create cute art like Moriah. There are many funny people. There are many excellent video editors, certainly some who may have more professional capacity.

Yet, most are frustrated from not making a comfortable and fun living out of their talent. In their mind, "It's not possible, so why bother?"

That's why there are millions of talented people who are not following their purpose, and there is only one Moriah who makes an estimated millions by combining her best talents.

Fortune favors the bold in any industry.

This Bad Bitch Became Her Own Genre

Spanish singer and songwriter, Rosalía, exudes high magnetism and powerhouse main character energy. Her music is a blend of genres in a way that has never been done before.

Her early passion for flamenco as a teenager led her to receive formal training, a master's degree in the art form. She tried for years to make it as a flamenco singer, but the struggles of a starving artist ensued. She played at backyard parties, often receiving dinner or a small fee in exchange for her performance.

While still in school, in 2018, she released an interesting record called *El mal querer,* a unique blend of flamenco, pop, and urban music. This record was completely self-funded, recorded in one of her mentor's apartments with a computer, a microphone, and a sound table. She later described that funding this project made her almost bankrupt.

The record was a huge audacious risk, as there had been no similar genre or sound mix in the music world. Until this point, flamenco, pop, and reggaeton mixes had never been done before. Rosalía's creation was an artful blend of genres of music that normally don't go together, while maintaining the integrity of each genre. She combined flamenco, a sophisticated but unpopular music form, with reggaeton, which is a trendy, best-selling popular urban music genre.

This unexpected combination became an unexpected hit.

Since that record, Rosalía's struggling artist story became history.

It took her 15 years to find a unique style that blended her years of flamenco studies with her interest in popular and urban music, and while this combination could have gone horribly wrong, it shot her into incredible stardom as famous celebrities took note of her audacious, unique, and passionate music. Her music went viral on social media.

As a consequence, her album won her many awards, including four at the prestigious Latin Grammy Awards. Since then, she has released collaborations with countless famous artists in both Spanish and English-speaking music scenes.

Within a span of only five years, Rosalía, who was going bankrupt when she bet on herself with everything she had to make her breakthrough record, became a worldwide best-selling artist with an estimated worth of $50 million.

She, of course, wouldn't be the whole package without her charismatic sex appeal.

The Bad Bitch always has sex appeal. This does not only refer to conventional sexiness. It's an energy, a magnetic life force that sucks you in. It consumes your attention. It's an inexplicable attraction that is a combination of audaciousness, unbotheredness, and undeniable talent. She always rides the waves of trends. Her presence and creations give you excitement and energy. You get sucked into her world. She's attractive even to those who aren't normally interested in her industry or art form.

That sexiness is her magnetic charisma. She is authentic and unapologetically shines bright to be seen.

It's the exact kind of vibe, attitude, and presence that would make trolls say, "Who does she think she is?"

The Bad Bitch smiles and waves back.

While the troll yells, "Who the fuck do you think you are? What you're doing makes no sense! You're nothing!"

The Bad Bitch, in her cool, calm, peaceful prowess, gently reveals her next project. It's so cool that her audience loves her even more!

While the Bad Bitch is flying, the Good Girl is stuck because she's surrounded by rigid, inauthentic, boring, fearful, risk-averse individuals. Her perception of reality and what is possible is shaped by these people's realities.

You keep doing the same thing, expecting different results. You only try what's realistic based on the people around you who don't even understand your ambition. You're so consumed by fear that you live within the limitations of this shell. No matter how brightly you try to shine, you end up feeling defeated.

The Bad Bitch is a unique combination of a realist and a dreamer.

She pays attention to the aspects of her that people are most excited by and answers that call. She uses every gift she has. She makes that magnetism a part of her ambition. A blend of more than one unique qualities make her a standout main character. She bets on herself to expand, over and over again.

Her audacity is her daring to shine to be seen and a blend of her unique gifts and qualities. This is her gold, her winning formula, and it's only a matter of time before she claims this treasure.

She makes it happen.

CHAPTER TEN

Endurance

Turn pain into curiosity and fun.

The Bad Bitch looks like an overnight success, but she is not. If you really look deeply, she spent many years committing herself to her craft.

If you look closely into Moriah Elizabeth's journey, it took her years of posting on YouTube to find the right formula. No doubt that meanwhile, she endured disappointments and "failed projects."

Rosalía's story isn't only about audaciousness. Her story represents what every powerful and successful Bad Bitch possesses, which is endurance. It took her 15 years to find her unique artistry, and during that time, she bore all types of struggles.

Most influencers, artists, authors, and entrepreneurs share similar journeys.

The Bad Bitch is committed to her ambition, and with that commitment comes endurance.

She is mature, and therefore she knows that she's in for an ultra-long marathon, and not a sprint.

She's in for the long game.

She's in, no matter what.

Her mindset says, "I'm going to go hard until I find out what my potential really is."

She has conviction.

There's no way that she will leave this life without knowing what it is really about.

When it doesn't work out, she finds new solutions.

She is determined to find a way to make it happen.

When it gets hard, she finds satisfaction in learning and progressing.

Success is a puzzle for her. She leans in with curiosity to find the right answer.

This is *doing what it takes.*

The Good Girl is naïve.

She has dreams, but she doesn't know what it takes.

She avoids hard things in life. She avoids disappointment. She doesn't want to "waste effort," not realizing that this is how you polish your competence.

She gets excited when she finds her purpose and expects everything to work out for her immediately.

She gets frustrated when reality doesn't reflect instant success.

She dreams of being "found" by someone.

She wants to be saved from hard work.

She makes excuses when she sees other successful people.

She tries for a bit, but when her meager efforts don't give her immediate gratification with money, recognition, or even likes on social media, she loses motivation and stops.

This is the opposite of how the Bad Bitch approaches life and goals.

If you look at every successful Bad Bitch, they were in for the long haul.

The Bad Bitch knows there is no shortcut to success.

Endurance is a requirement for everyone.

It takes an average of five years of daily practice to build decent competence, and ten years to reach Mastery in that skill.

That's why giving up on your ambition because it's not working is not an option.

When you see a young successful Bad Bitch, it means she found her strength and started honing it from very early in her life. Many start honing their skills as tots and reach success in their teens or early 20s. That's about ten or more years.

There are no exceptions to this rule.

The Bad Bitch success can be found at any age; however, endurance is a habit, and many adults struggle to build a habit they were never disciplined to embody in childhood.

If this is you, you must start now.

When you hit roadblocks, know that failure is when you learn the most. Use those times to refine your craft.

When you have limitations, this is when you become the most creative. Sharpen your creativity.

When you keep failing, become the gritty Bad Bitch and find a better solution.

Just stick with it, knowing that every overnight success took more than ten years of hard work.

THIS BAD BITCH'S OVERNIGHT SUCCESS TOOK TWO DECADES

Viola Davis is a beautiful and talented actress who came from an extremely impoverished background. She made it to Juilliard School for Drama and graduated in 1993.

This, in itself, was a miracle, because Juilliard is a prestigious school often only accessible for the wealthy.

Despite having found her true pathway and polishing her undeniable talent in acting since a very young age, she struggled to find significant roles in Hollywood early in her career.

For many years, she worked in theater and appeared in various television shows and movies in supporting roles. During this time, she was paying her bills with a lot of difficulty. She often faced limited opportunities and typecasting due to Hollywood's lack of diverse and substantial roles for women of color.

Most people would have given up, gotten a secure job, and quit on this uncertain pathway that seemed to have little future opportunities, but Viola knew this was her pathway and was fully committed to her ambition.

It wasn't until 2008, 15 years after graduating from Juilliard, when she was cast in a supporting role in the critically acclaimed film *Doubt*, that her talents began to gain more recognition. Her powerful performance alongside Meryl Streep and Philip Seymour Hoffman earned her an Academy Award nomination for Best Supporting Actress.

However, it was her role as Aibileen Clark in the 2011 film *The Help* that catapulted her to stardom. Her portrayal of a strong and resilient African-American maid in the racially charged 1960s earned her widespread acclaim and another Academy Award nomination, this time for Best Actress.

In 2015, Viola won the Academy Award for Best Supporting Actress for her role in *Fences*, making history as the first black woman to achieve the Triple Crown of Acting (winning an Oscar, Emmy, and Tony).

Viola Davis's journey to success serves as an example of perseverance and talent, her endurance to prevail against the odds.

After almost two decades of facing initial struggles and limited opportunities in Hollywood, she persevered, honed her craft, and eventually emerged as one of the most respected and celebrated actresses of her generation.

Look deeply into any Bad Bitch's journey. Any scale of success follows the same format.

She finds her strength and goes all-in, and if she isn't quickly taking off, she's investing her time, energy, and money, honing her talent to emerge as one of the best.

Uncertainty could make her quit, yet she invested over a decade into her craft, her ambition.

Viola spent over two decades becoming a master, yet she made it look so glamorous and effortless that she created an illusion of an overnight success.

CHAPTER ELEVEN

Harnessing Sexual Energy

**Your life force energy is the source of your
spirituality, creativity, and healing nurture.**

D esire, which is the power behind ambition, comes from sexual energy.

Sexual energy is a powerful life force. Throughout history, numerous creative and successful men have drawn inspiration from their muses to fuel their ambitions. They transmuted their powerful sexual urge to channel and to create their best work and inventions.

Under patriarchy, women's sexuality has been controlled under scrutiny. Taking away sexual power is taking away her life force and ambition. By patriarchal standards, there is no way she can be Good, even when she tries. She is a prude or a slut. She's a mother or a whore. She's a Good Girl or a Bitch.

This is the definition of oppression.

The word "bitch" comes from what you'd call a female dog. This word dates back to the 15th century and was used against women deemed to be too sexually open, as female dogs give birth to many puppies. An equivalent term for a man is a bastard. Even this term insults his mother's sexual habits more than it insults her son. Her sexuality is always a problem.

No matter what, her sexuality must center around men. Women today are still navigating the world with this oppressed mindset. This is why hook-up culture isn't feminism. It's a form of oppression. It only benefits men, to have fun without taking on any responsibility or accountability, while she carries most of the risks of being contaminated by diseases, getting pregnant, and suffering potential slut shaming.

A woman has to be very careful in navigating the landmine of shame that can blast towards her in an instant. Sexually shaming and labeling are rampant and rule social media, school bullying, and life in general. A woman's greatest fear has been rape or sextortion, to be threatened to release her intimate videos and photos. That's why protective people say to a woman, "You could have been killed or *worse*," referring to some kind of sexual crime done to her, which is considered worse than her death.

Women's sexuality has been used as a weapon against them, and women have learned to adopt default coping mechanisms.

There are two types of Good Girls when it comes to sexuality, and both are types of "personality" developed from coping mechanisms to deal with patriarchal oppression, objectification, and/or sexual abuse:

1. The Suppressed

   Patriarchy trained her to feel shame around her sexuality. She deeply believes that it is a bad thing. She is embarrassed of sexuality. She claims that she has little to no libido and doesn't have much interest in sex. When she has sex, it's to reproduce or to appease and satisfy her partner.

She self-validates with sexual morals and purity, so she can judge women who exude sexual energy. This is how she can be Good.

2. The Pick-Me

She learned to use the male gaze to her advantage. She learned through observation and experience that appealing to what men want gives her attention, societal validation, and even helps her get ahead. In this process, she's constantly competing with other women.

She believes that she's highly sexual, loves sex, and goes over the top with expressing male-approved versions of female sexuality. She wants to show the world that she's the best, she is chosen, and that she's an inspiring free woman.

Both the Suppressed and the Pick-Me are one and the same. They're both naïve. While they may not have the words to describe their own condition, they are both reacting from the same place of helplessness. They are both making desperate attempts to cope and survive under the oppressive patriarchal condition.

What both types of the Good Girls are unable to see clearly is that they are both anti-feminists and anti-women. In reality, they are pro-patriarchy, and unwittingly, through their conduct, are enabling the oppression of women.

With the Suppressed, desexualization is infantilization. She is not a woman with desires. She's a controllable child. She learned to use sex only as an exclusive service to her partner, which keeps the relationship harmonious and gives her protection and security.

With the Pick-Me, oversexualization is fetishization. She's not a woman. She's an object of pleasure for men. She competes against other women. Nobody can be better than her. She has other Pick-Mes that look up to her and want to be just like her. That's why many Pick-Mes are very good social media influencers. They sell their fellow women products and services on how to be a better Pick-Me for the male gaze: anti-aging products, waist-cinchers, cosmetic procedures, and even trying dangerous methods to stay unrealistically young.

The Pick-Me learned to trade her sexuality as a bartering tool in a patriarchal society, further perpetuating and promoting the objectification of women. She is benefiting from, and therefore reinforcing the patriarchal agenda that objectifies women as eye candy and pleasure givers.

The Good Girl is easy to spot, as she has defining symptoms when it comes to her body and sexuality:

♦ She is obsessively concerned about her looks.

♦ She has bad posture, either to hide her body or to accentuate her female body parts, such as overextending her lower back to puff up her chest and stick out her butt to look more curvy (the Pick-Me pose).

♦ She only feels sexual during the chase and the foreplay.

♦ As soon as the sex begins, or when she has the partner committed, she loses interest because she is turned on by validation and not the sex.

♦ She uses sexual openness to hide her insecurities.

- She has an internalized male gaze that is constantly evaluating her own fashion, style, and behavioral choice and judges other women from that standard.

- For young Good Girls, they embody sexual facial expressions and suggestive body language that they learned through porn culture, perpetuated by the Pick-Me influencers on social media.

The sad truth is that both the Suppressed and the Pick-Me Good Girls are disconnected from their sexuality.

The Good Girl who claims to be sexual hasn't even recently looked inside her vulva, nor noticed which one of her breasts hangs lower. She lives in a rush. Her showers are done quickly. Looking at her body carefully brings up so much shame that she automatically avoids it, unless she's feeling masochistic to brutally criticize and scrutinize herself in front of the mirror or on the scale.

The Good Girl is uncomfortable with her body and her sexuality.

She is self-rejecting.

This is why you struggle with your self-esteem.

When the Good Girl is lonely and coping by herself, she shouts, "Women supporting women!" She wants support. What she's really saying here is, "Women, please support me! I lack nurture and have done everything to kill my femininity and my authenticity to appeal to men. I'm traumatized, miserable, and have no peace."

The patriarchally brainwashed Good Girl mindset can't reciprocate "Women Supporting Women." She's a giver to her oppressor and a taker to those who are capable of helping. She feels the need to be better and to be the chosen one, to feel that she's enough.

She can't bear anyone being better than her. To live her standards, there can be no collaboration, only competition.

This is why the Good Girl doesn't have real friends. No matter how nice she is, she eventually makes other women feel bad because she needs to be the best. This is why the Good Girl can never be an ally for the Bad Bitch. She allies with men because when she does just the right things, pleasing and validating them takes her to places.

This is another layer of your glass ceiling. As you start becoming more competent, as you become less naïve, as you start holding him accountable, or as your patriarchy-approved pretty privilege starts fading, he starts to become lukewarm and mechanical towards you, and eventually stops helping you. At this point, you've dug your own grave to have no solidarity with women, and now the answer isn't so simple as to go for men's support. The patriarchally entitled men have already left the scene to search for better eye candy and a new source of nurture, ease, and convenience.

The Good Girl misuses her sexual energy because she doesn't understand its tremendous power.

Your sexual energy is blocked with shame and guilt from watching the women in your life experience marital pains and betrayals. You experienced sexual abuse, or at least early objectification, and come from a sex-negative upbringing. To cope, you blocked out your emotions.

Doing so, you are blocked from having a spiritual relationship with yourself.

You are blocked from your intuition, which is why you notice that your intuition is accurate sometimes, but at other times, leads you to make detrimental decisions.

You have blocked creativity, which is why your creations don't yield the results you want, and why you can't figure out the right solutions.

You are blocked from generating and receiving nurture, which is your self-healing energy. This is why you keep self-sabotaging.

The Good Girl doesn't understand the value of her sexual energy.

You give away your power to those who don't value you. You care more about what's in your smoothie than the quality of the person that enters your body.

You chase validation and convenience with your sexuality. You chain date and obsess over someone who doesn't show the love and care that you deserve.

When you finally get the man in bed, you want to "get it over and done with."

Your fragmented sexuality becomes an ongoing distraction and a sabotage for you.

1. Sleeping with the enemy.

   You choose to be with a partner who doesn't understand your value and potential. You put your wellness, safety, and potential at risk.

   You even reproduce with them, which becomes a huge financial suicide. This commitment can last from 18 years to a lifetime, depending on the needs of your children. Imagine the ongoing struggle to have a lifelong project with someone who doesn't respect you. Imagine all the stress, lost opportunities, and potential in that time.

The Good Girl claims to have learned her lesson when she ends a bad relationship. She says, "I claimed myself through my breakup." Yet, she has a series of relapses and keeps making the same mistakes over and over again.

You claim that your ambitions matter the most, yet the next minute, you're hitting up exes, swiping left and right, and even considering having a baby with the man you thought about breaking up with just five minutes ago.

2. Childbearing for the wrong reasons.

You want children so you can feel love, not realizing that childbearing is a position of service to the children. It's a selfless and not a self-fulfilling act. You needing love is selfish and the absolute wrong reason to have them. This intention becomes the beginning of your children's trauma. Having kids doesn't make you love yourself more.

When using your children as a source of validation doesn't fill your own lovelessness, you chase a new source of validation while neglecting your children. You do this by becoming a workaholic or obsessing over a man. You make your children's lives the reason you can't conveniently live the way you want. If the relationship with their father doesn't work out, the children become the source of your problems, as they're the reason why you're still tied to the wrong partner, their father. This is how the Good Girl perpetuates the generational curse. Consequently, you pass on your self-love deficit to your children, burdening them with shame just for existing.

You don't become the Bad Bitch until you upgrade your relationship with your sexuality.

This begins with having self-control.

This doesn't necessarily mean abstinence. It's about understanding the power of your sexual energy and channeling it well.

To do that, you need to work on releasing false beliefs and the shameful emotions that rule your automatically ingrained patriarchal sexual behaviors. Sex is not a barter tool. It's a sacred force.

When you have self-control, you use your sexual energy to create your best work.

You practice sex as a spiritually elevating ritual with a deserving partner who understands your value.

The Bad Bitch was once a Good Girl who learned to value and harness her sexual energy for creativity, productivity, and self-nurturing.

That's why there is only one type of Bad Bitch when it comes to sexuality.

She isn't triggered by sex, use it to prove herself, or make it her identity.

She values, owns, and enjoys her sexual power.

She has an elegant allure. She carries herself confidently. She is physically healthy, relaxed, and is kinetically aware.

She glides in her movements.

She dresses modestly and elegantly.

She has style.

How you carry yourself is an expression of your sexual energy.

Even with a $5 T-shirt, the Bad Bitch looks, feels, and smells expensive.

Her stride is confident, her body language is self-assured, and she speaks confidently, concisely, and assertively.

Her magnetic charisma comes from being at ease with every part of herself, including her sexuality.

The Bad Bitch doesn't talk sexually or look sexual, but she spends plenty of time looking at her own body. She appreciates it, knowing that in just a moment in time, her body will change and look different again.

She spends time before each shower looking at her body, caressing it, and gently gazing at her bare face, her collarbone, the curves of her waist, the roundness of her butt, and the changing landscape of her vulva.

She has a creative and fun-loving relationship with her pleasure. This is why she's good in bed. She prioritizes her pleasure for herself. Think Samantha from *Sex and the City* and her fun-loving attitude toward sex. It makes sense that Samantha, who has a comfortable relationship with her sexuality, is the wealthiest and the most accomplished character. She's a true boss lady.

The Bad Bitch's deep appreciation for her body and her sexuality is the secret portal to her spirituality, limitless creativity, and healing energy. It's the source of her abundance.

Your healing process starts with the process of appreciation.

You hold space for how much your body has served you through various growths, trauma, and life transitions. This appreciation is self-respect. It's healing. It makes space for your relationship with pleasure to flourish.

As you heal your spiritual relationship with yourself, you open up the channel to turn your sexual urges into creativity.

When you feel the sexual urge, instead of releasing it through an impatient orgasm or using it to shapeshift yourself into becoming a better Pick-Me, do the following to expand your creativity and productivity.

1. When you feel the urge, hold the sexual energy in your pelvic area.

2. With each breath, visualize moving the energy up your spine, up to your brain, and experience an explosion of creativity and mental clarity.

3. This creativity is what deepens your connection to spirituality, what you may call the downloads from the Source or the Universe, where you get your ideas from.

4. Holding this creative energy, channel it to produce the most creative and hardest parts of your life's work.

5. The creation process in this state has a nurturing and healing effect on your soul, which others will feel too when they come in contact with your energy, either by being around you or through your work.

6. The more you harness your sexual energy for creativity and productivity, the bigger the energy gets, and this is how you reach Mastery.

This process initiates spiritual upgrades. You experience bliss and flow, a state of deep immersion and focus, where you create incredible work within very little time.

This is how you become creative, productive, exciting, and nurturing all at the same time. The creative process regenerates you as much as you generate healing energy for others.

This is the state of energetic abundance.

This nurturing energy is very peaceful. You feel secure. You feel good about yourself, so you can make space for others to grow together and to collaborate.

Healing your sexuality is part of the metamorphic completion to become the Bad Bitch because every Bad Bitch is creative, spiritual, and nurturing. She is an alchemist who transmutes her sexual energy to create her best work, backed by this powerful life force energy.

When you meet the Bad Bitch, she feels very healing. She is an ally to those who are growth-minded, respectful, and committed to their greatest potential. As you upgrade from the Good Girl to become the Bad Bitch, you recognize her, and she becomes your trustworthy ally. Even when you ally with one Bad Bitch, you become a part of a real nurturing and supportive community because it takes two to start a community. Not to mention, the experienced Bad Bitch already has a network with those similar to her.

Sexual energy is the source of ever-flowing happiness, peace, and creative ideas that produce fulfillment and financial abundance.

It's freedom.

Sexual energy alchemy is a self-nurturing and self-generating, self-healing nurture cycle that emanates to lift and heal others.

CHAPTER TWELVE

Clairsenses

Intuition is the North Star that guides you through confusion.

When you're healed and open, your spirituality enhances, and your intuition heightens.

You become connected with the Source or the Universe. You can receive guidance, which often consists of thoughts or visions to appear in your mind.

This is why the Bad Bitch feels like a magician. How she reads your mind isn't magic. It's enlightened intuition.

There are four most common types of intuition, collectively known as the *clair*, meaning *light* in French. Depending on your spiritual and genetic makeup, although you naturally leverage all four types of intuition, you may develop to become more in tune with a specific form of intuition.

1. **Clairvoyance**, the ability to *see* visions and images before they come true.

2. **Claircognizance**, the ability to just *know* the truth.

3. **Clairaudience**, *hearing* guiding sounds.

4. **Clairsentient**, the ability to *feel* beyond what's visible.

The Good Girl lives in survival mode. She lives in fear.

She believes that she's very intuitive, but what she actually experiences most of the time is instinct.

Her true gut feelings are buried underneath the many layers of fear.

Her instinct is often hypervigilance, the constant worry that there are dangerous threats in her environment. She can't stop from being constantly alert that something may go horribly wrong at any given time.

The Good Girl never felt safe as a child, and therefore she's been on constant alert her whole life. She's still doing the same as an adult.

This is why you can't enjoy life.

You're numb and can't *feel*. You have moments of good intuition, but most of what you feel is instinct. That's why you're so confused as to why your intuition sometimes seems to work, and at other times, it gets you into serious problems. You can't trust yourself.

Intuition, like wisdom, becomes refined with experience, knowledge, and emotional intelligence. It does not follow calculated logic. Typically, real intuitive downloads don't make much logical sense. It feels inconvenient to follow. It feels unrealistic, uncomfortable, out of reach, and you can't comprehend why you're getting these downloads.

When you see an intuitive image or a vision, you can't see all the steps of *how* or *when* you'll create the outcome into reality.

The Good Girl gets overwhelmed here, so she doesn't follow through, even when she gets the intuitive answers that she's been asking for.

Your clairsenses can only be tapped in when you embody safety and trust in your body.

You trust what you are shown and you flow with it. You don't have to know *how*. You just have to start where you are.

You can only trust when you already feel safe.

You don't control your intuition or try to make it make sense based on your limited perception. Needing to control the outcome is what makes it instinctual, and you end up making the wrong decision.

Clairsenses, or true intuition, feel like this:

- ◆ It's a pressing feeling to take a particular action without any apparent reason, even when it goes against logic, expectations, and conventions.
- ◆ You keep getting the sense, hearing, seeing, or feeling the same thing, over and over again.
- ◆ The urge hits you when you least expect it.

Everyone is born with clairsenses. As a child, you were trained to not trust yourself, so you stopped listening.

The Bad Bitch had to heal her trust issues to regain access to her incredible intuition. She healed her coping mechanisms, found out who she really was, and emotionally unblocked herself to experience a high level of spiritual freedom.

Feeling safe opens your creativity channel, which allows the mind to open up to *possibilities* beyond circumstantial limitations and mental blocks.

This is why the Bad Bitch's most dangerous, protective, and reliable power is her intuition.

This is why you can't lie to her. Even when you're good, she'll know you're lying.

She has so much trust within herself that projection, manipulation, and blame tactics don't work on her.

When the Bad Bitch has a goal or a need, her clairsenses guide her towards the right pathway.

Feeling safe is what allows her to take that chance.

She chooses the right people to ally with, finds herself at the right place at the right time, and makes lucrative money moves.

How Leaving a Date Made Me $7,000

A man I met through mutual friends asked me out on a date. This happened a few years after I gave back that platinum and diamond ring to that ex-boyfriend. I certainly wasn't looking for a relationship after I committed to a non-committal Bad Bitch lifestyle, and my life and business were going well.

After pondering whether I should let myself get distracted from building my own business and leading my family, something within me said "yes" when he asked me to meet at a cafe in East Vancouver.

I wasn't interested in the date itself, but I felt a strong pull to visit that neighborhood. Could it be familiarity? I lived in that neighborhood in my early 20s. I felt an uplifting excitement, so I agreed.

It was a busy neighborhood with barely any parking. When I arrived, I found a parking spot immediately. Was this a good sign for the date or a good sign for something else? It didn't matter. I was open to finding out what this feeling was about.

As my gut initially indicated to me, the date wasn't stimulating. There was no way I could even consider dating a man who had never gone to therapy in his life and was unaware that his fun "stories" were actually trauma-dumping. (After this incident, I always do initial Zoom calls to screen people before meeting in person.)

Within 30 minutes, shortly after we started sharing a conversation, I started to feel myself tuning out. Right then, I felt a sudden urge in my gut to leave. I thanked him for the matcha oat milk latte, told him that I was not feeling a connection, and left.

The old Good Girl me could never. I would have felt bad! As the Bad Bitch, I felt so certain that I had to get out of there because there was another wondrous energy waiting for me.

My car was parked in a surprisingly silent area in a sidestreet, in a normally bustling neighborhood. I felt a sudden urge from my gut to record a video. I could have been influenced by being in my old neighborhood and tapping into the older version of how I used to be. I talked about how I used to have an intense fear of speaking up, and that was what was holding me back from starting on my ambition. After almost seven years of fighting with myself, I talked about how I started a YouTube channel back in 2012, only to delete it all within a few months. I spoke about my transformational process and my discoveries of how my childhood had an impact on the stubborn mental blocks around self-expression. There was no script. My speech flowed in a flawless delivery. The sun hit me just in the right place, making me glow better than using any filter. The background was beautiful. I was walking, coincidentally passing by the social media management company Hootsuite's head office.

Once that video was posted, it started to go viral. I immediately had an audience member reach out to me, via a private message. I answered. We kept going back and forth until I asked her if she wanted to have a call. We had a call on the spot. I sat in my car to have more privacy. We discussed a combination of coaching and consulting, which resulted in a $7,000 business deal, paid and closed on the spot. I had other leads from the same video too. That one video generated five figures for me.

Stuck in that boring date, getting depleted in a conversation I didn't want to be having, giving away my energy, time, and nurture for *free* to someone who hasn't done anything for me? For what? To be seen as a good person?

No thanks.

Many people have asked me over the years how I managed to make a living as a coach, whether that's even a real job, especially because most people who are a part of this billion-dollar industry can't make a living out of it. Only the top 3% do, but that's the nature of being in any business, period.

The Bad Bitch's intuition leads her to a higher vibration. The Good Girl instinct does attempt to get in the way, but where would I be if I didn't listen to my senses?

Following through on a simple intuitive hit can become your next big money move, how you meet your business partner, a significant influencer or a friend, or even a life-giving love partner.

You have to feel safe to trust, then follow through.

THIS BAD BITCH'S INTUITION WAS WORTH BILLIONS

In 1998, while getting ready for a party, Sara Blakely became frustrated by the lack of comfortable and flattering undergarments to wear under white pants.

She wondered if she could create something like pantyhose but without the feet, to create a streamlined silhouette that doesn't show her panty line under white pants.

To test out her idea, she bought a pair of pantyhose and cut the feet off, and it did the job for her! She wore it under her white pants and the pantyhose amazingly held her curves the right way.

She wondered if she could make this and sell it.

She hemmed and hawed on this idea, as she didn't have any experience in fashion or business. She only had $5,000 in savings. There was no way that would be enough to fund a brand-new business in a completely unfamiliar industry.

Two years before, Sara said to herself that one day, she'd like to create a product that would help millions of people, but she didn't know what that could be.

She didn't know that this problem she had with white pants, and the pantyhose without feet, could be that idea.

The idea made no logical sense to her to pursue it as a business, but she kept seeing the image of pantyhose without feet. Yet, there was no product like this in the market.

Surely, the people who specialize in fashion know better than someone like her, who was a fax machine salesperson. If they knew better, why would there be no such product in the market already?

To clear her confusion and indecision, she asked for a sign.

One day, she turned on the TV, and it was *The Oprah Winfrey Show*. In this particular episode, Oprah said something along the lines of, "Why don't they make pantyhose without the feet?"

Sara was flabbergasted. This had to be the sign she was asking for. She couldn't question it anymore. She had to just trust and go.

With no experience in fashion or business, she followed her intuition every step of the way.

She began experimenting with different materials to create a prototype for what would become the first pair of Spanx shapewear. It was initially a challenge to even get a factory to take her and her idea seriously enough to make her product, but she used her persistence and persuasion from her sales career to finally make it happen.

She used her intuitive senses to refine the product, ensuring that it would meet the needs of women like herself.

In 2000, Sara Blakely introduced Spanx to the market. Initially, she faced numerous rejections from retail stores, but she believed in the product and remained true to her intuition. Her senses told her to keep going, so she did.

Her intuition was right.

Oprah Winfrey featured Spanx on *The Oprah Winfrey Show*, giving the brand significant exposure. This led to a surge in demand, and Spanx quickly became a global sensation.

Intuition was the start of a company that now has reached over a billion dollars.

CHAPTER THIRTEEN

The Subconscious Mind

An abundant mindset is your freedom.

T he Good Girl's mindset is set on scarcity programming.
Experiencing lack is her comfort zone, and that's why she continuously chooses people who don't give her enough time, care, and validation.

The Good Girl dates down. She friendships down. She settles in her career choice, when choosing a lover, and in her pay too.

She prioritizes being Good. In patriarchal terms, that's not having needs. It's self-propagated depletion.

Subconsciously, she never feels like she's enough, and therefore, she settles for what never gives her enough.

Meanwhile, she destroys herself with work. She lives in a constant state of fight or flight, working hard to escape an imagined vision of doom.

Comfort, nurture, and leisure are concepts far from her reality.

She wants to experience a life of surplus and abundance, yet, her scarcity mental programming directs her to choose depleting options because that's what's familiar for her.

The Bad Bitch calibrates her mindset to standardize abundance.

She prioritizes the feeling of having more than enough resources and only considers relationship offers that meet her needs.

Earning more money than she needs, keeping, and growing her wealth is a familiar standard.

Evaluating to keep only valuable and contributing relationships is a default habit.

Experiencing joy, leisure, happiness, and wonder are daily musts for her.

The Bad Bitch's mindset is programmed to prioritize surplus, and therefore, she feels that she's more than enough.

Reprogramming your subconscious is the key to your elevation.

You do not live with free will.

All your thinking, feelings, experiencing, decision-making, and action-taking are controlled by your subconscious, which has been programmed through the observations and experiences in your childhood.

When you say, "I didn't see that coming," forces that cannot be detected with your thinking mind have been leading you to this outcome.

This remains true until you train yourself to develop the mind's eye to see what isn't possible to be seen by the untrained mind.

The subconscious mind does not follow the logic of your conscious, thinking mind. It's your emotional mind and your habits center.

Your subconscious programming's purpose is to help you navigate and survive this world better, based on your childhood and family experiences.

Your subconscious programming has been set by the age of 10, which becomes the foundation of your coping mechanisms and automatic reactions in thinking, experiencing, feeling, and acting.

Your adult life decisions are based on this foundational survival programming.

The Good Girl struggle is this: your pleaser and shape-shifting coping mechanisms have helped you survive your childhood environment, and now, the same programming is no longer helping you thrive, primarily in your trauma-based interpretations and the fear-based reactions.

The Bad Bitch is an expert in the workings of the human subconscious.

What the subconscious mind wants is to keep experiencing what feels familiar because there's comfort in certainty.

Your subconscious will override your goals and willpower if it isn't a match to what your subconscious mind wants, which is familiarity.

This is why you keep repeating experiences from the past.

This is why you face a challenge when leveling up.

No matter what you want to achieve, your subconscious takes you back to a default standard of living.

If your millionaire dream, fame, big accolades, and even the loving, supportive partner and friendships that you want aren't cataloged in your subconscious as a familiar experience for your survival, there are no data records of such experiences.

No matter your goals, your mind will direct you away from these goals and take you toward what will give you certainty based on your past experiences.

Familiarity is favored because certainty and predictability *feels safe*.

The desire for safety bypasses your degrees, logic, and intelligence in the decision-making process.

Your subconscious will keep directing you toward the familiar emotional experiences that you've experienced in your life. The subconscious is the root reason why you observe recurring issues and even traumatic experiences.

The Bad Bitch breaks generational cycles and achieves great success such as fame, fortune, and a healthy and happy lifestyle and relationships because she reprograms her subconscious to familiarize and standardize abundance.

THE PROVEN 7-STEP PROCESS TO REPROGRAMMING YOUR SUBCONSCIOUS

1. Envision what you want in detail.

   Detailed envisioning leads to the feeling of being in a movie of your future self. It makes the desired outcome feel vivid and within reach.

2. You must immerse yourself in the environment that you desire.

   If it's wealth, you have to immerse yourself in wealthy experiences where you're immersed in a luxurious environment. To improve your relationships, you must surround yourself with mature, emotionally intelligent individuals.

3. Feeling safe is key.

    What you feel matters. If you immerse yourself in luxury while feeling anxious and worried, your subconscious will connect wealth with worry, which can potentially stop you from accumulating wealth, or you'll create wealth and the anxiety will make sure that you never have a moment of rest. You can potentially end up getting rid of your wealth to get rid of the anxiety. To prevent this, make your desired environment experience relaxing, peaceful, and safe.

4. Feel inspired.

    Once you feel safe, you can truly feel inspired by the vision of what you want because from the state of peace, you increase your emotional capacity. This is where you feel that you can make greater successes happen.

5. Take action.

    When you see an inspiring outcome within reach, take congruent actions to turn that into reality. Gather the right knowledge, resources, and take the right action steps to make it happen. Keep adjusting and putting in the work until you get the outcome that matches your inspired vision.

6. Confirmation.

    When you experience the right results, your mind experiences reward and relief. That satisfying experience releases happy hormones, which signify to your mind that this is indeed the right experience for you to survive better. You win over your subconscious mind's approval to make wealth and healthy choices a standard.

7. Repetition.

    The satisfying feedback causes you to repeat the whole process, which builds your achiever identity. You know that you're the Bad Bitch that creates opportunities and wealth.

    The Bad Bitch's identity is that she's an achiever, a fantastic decision-maker, and an alchemizer. Every Bad Bitch, whether she was aware of the exact steps or not, starts out on her success journey following the seven aforementioned steps.

This Bad Bitch Upgraded to Freedom

When I first met Lydia, she was working 12 hours a day for 7 days a week on her business, generating around $30,000 a month. As a single woman, she had deleted everything in her life to prioritize her financial wealth, but the chase to success had left her depleted, exhausted, and, to her shock, suicidal.

Lydia started her business like most entrepreneurs. She wanted to be free from a boss that micromanaged her. She got tired of getting a $5,000 raise every few years. She wanted to escape and have freedom, yet now she found herself without any discipline around her working hours, hustling non-stop.

She shared that she felt so much fear that she couldn't stop working. She felt that she would hit poverty or ruin herself if she gave herself breaks. She had control issues and couldn't properly delegate to staff. It felt like too much of a risk for her. Although she was unaware until I mentioned it, her exhaustion largely came from micromanaging her staff.

Lydia came from a neglectful family that didn't ever prioritize wellness. Both of her parents had been workaholics and weren't ever available. They never looked after their bodies and were very un-healthy in their elderly years.

Lydia demonstrated similar patterns in her adult life. She was over-worked as a student and in every job she had. After overworking for two decades, she was on the verge of breaking down. Her body was unhealthy, and, only in her mid-thirties, she could barely walk up a set of stairs without panting.

Lydia was overwhelmed by the fear of doom, poverty, death, and even success. She couldn't stop working because being lazy was a bad thing in her family. As a child, she was never given a moment of rest. She was constantly pushed by her parents to be actively doing something, like studying, practicing an instrument, or doing chores. She was under a constant invisible pressure to be *useful.*

While she was overworking to become financially successful, she was afraid of not being liked and being seen as a bad person if she succeeded.

Lydia had a hard time defining what her goals were. I helped ease her into the idea that peace and leisure were good goals to have. There was no way that in her current mental, emotional, and phys-ical state, she could reach her ambition. She had desires to have a social life, but she also felt afraid of it.

For the first time in her life, Lydia stopped chasing and worked on attracting peace and abundance into her life.

I got her started in the process of upgrading her to embody a sur-plus, abundant mindset by helping her create an honest vision.

With difficulty, she admitted that she did deeply want to have an easier life, but she felt guilty admitting to this due to her childhood experiences and the opinions of her parents about laziness that kept ruminating in her mind. Peace and ease made her feel terribly guilty.

She wanted to eventually not work and have her business be run by her staff. Since she had a social media marketing agency, I told her that this was very simple to achieve.

First, Lydia and I set proper goals for her and categorized the type of delegation that made sense for each role. She had been delegating to her staff haphazardly, like throwing spaghetti on the wall. Her high anxiety often led to frustration when her staff didn't meet her unclear instructions, last-minute deadlines, and undiscussed expectations for random projects that seemed to come out of nowhere. Standardizing job descriptions, reviewing her communication skills, and sticking to clear and measurable parameters immediately stopped the toxic blaming cycle. This allowed the dust to settle, making the performance gaps clearly visible.

Second, the organized efficiency boosted the company's productivity and revenue. What made her truly happy, though, wasn't just the increase in revenue but also the peaceful feeling that came with it, along with the belief that this time, it would be *sustainable*.

Third, she needed to experience a life of peace, ease, and leisure. I had her go to the Fairmont Hotel to get a haircut, have a coffee, and swim in the facility. At first, she felt very uncomfortable. Coming from a humble, working-class background, she heard her parents' voices again, "Stop wasting your money!"

We worked on feeling safe in these luxurious environments by addressing the guilt and repairing and healing the lack of mindset with nurturing and inspiring thoughts.

Lydia was very open to change, and therefore, she changed very quickly. After only three times, she felt safer in these luxurious environments. She felt that she *belonged* there. She couldn't believe that she lived her whole life without feeling so alive and inspired. She joined the exercise club in the boutique gym and started working with a nutritionist. Through her nutritionist, she met other successful entrepreneurs like her, and her social life started to bloom.

Meanwhile, every day, she was working on her subconscious mind reprogramming process, and her congruent experiences were boosting the reprogramming much faster.

As she became healthier and happier, she found herself bombarded with creative thoughts, and her agency began to deliver better work than ever. Within the first month, she had already hired another staff member capable of handling much of the delivery work that she used to do. This freed up her time to focus on lead generation and meeting new prospective clients. Her new social environment gave her a boost of connections as well, where she gained many new clients through referrals. The most important part of her upgrade was firing the bad clients who were once happy to take advantage of the lesser version of her. They could not adjust to the new Lydia.

Lydia celebrated every new upgrade and win. Even her feeling good about herself and her new lifestyle were worthy of celebration. More and more, she started to feel certain that the way to success wasn't to overwork but to work less and to make more. She no longer feared laziness. She was proud of her new lifestyle. A life of peace and ease became a routine.

Her standards were raised to the point that within three months, she couldn't relate to who she was just a few months ago, struggling in her lowest, most unhealthy state, scrambling to make $30,000 a month while working for 12 hours a day, every single day of the week.

In the same time frame, Lydia hit over $150,000 a month in her agency with just one more staff to support the business expansion. By this point, she was working less than 20 hours a week.

All it took Lydia was to reprogram her subconscious mind to become a self-made millionaire, living a life of peace, ease, and happiness.

Chapter Fourteen

Outwitting the Scarcity Mindset

A poverty mindset is an urn with a broken bottom.

Reprogramming the subconscious is the sure way to reach your success, yet, even when given a proven process, you have a hard time leveling up in your life.

This is due to the scarcity mindset, which is a mindset that makes you innately human.

The scarcity mindset is often framed as a negative mindset, but this isn't true.

It is our survival programming. It's perfect for self-preservation and staying exactly where you are. It's the mindset that kept you safe all your life. This was very important in the days of our early ancestors, and even in our own childhoods.

The scarcity mindset only becomes an obstacle when you want to level up.

This mindset has been set by the time you were 10 years old, and unless you've been doing major mindset interventions, it's been ruling all your decision-making since.

This is your default life.

When you live based on your scarcity mindset, you will end up creating a replica version of your parents and your childhood experiences in your adult life. The longer you live, say, past 40 years old, this default life will become much more evident. This is why you'll find yourself saying, "I didn't want to, and I didn't think I would ever, but I'm acting exactly like my mom/dad!"

Scarcity mindset is felt as a state of depletion: Emotional exhaustion, lack of time, low self-worth, struggle, and net to subzero financial results. Health challenges, family conflict, and ongoing distress and depression are also scarcity symptoms.

Subconscious reprogramming is the key to change, yet that requires the Good Girl to bypass a huge mental obstacle.

Your biggest enemy on your pathway to becoming a Bad Bitch is your resistance.

♦ You inquire about change, feel better, and then do nothing more.

♦ You start but don't work consistently enough because you don't get immediate gratification, so you quit and return to your default life.

♦ You don't trust that it works because nobody in your family has ever opted into healing and upgrading their mindset.

♦ You can't get yourself to pay for your transformation because it's too expensive.

You often think that you don't have the money, but this isn't true because you have no trouble shopping, taking vacations, upgrading your phone, and even buying a fabulous bag. You have the wrong priorities, which means that you channel your resources into what feels good in the moment but doesn't help you break out of the self-deprecating Good Girl life.

The Good Girl is like Carrie Bradshaw from *Sex and the City*. When Carrie had to buy an apartment, she had no money left because she blew most of it on designer shoes.

Scarcity mindset is how you get stuck in the cycle of **addiction to struggle**.

Resistance is actually avoidance. What you're avoiding is feeling triggered. To outwit the scarcity state, you have to learn to face your triggers.

When the Good Girl gets triggered, she avoids. She impulsively quits, breaks up, ends a contract, and doesn't think about the *why* behind her actions.

When the Bad Bitch gets triggered, she stays with it. She steps up. She asks, "What's my own issue here? Is this actually bad for me so I need to leave it, or am I re-experiencing old pains through this experience?"

When triggers hit, the Good Girl gets righteous. She can't see her own problem in her own mess. She's the expert, more advanced, educated, smarter, richer, so she blames others. She's the victim. It must be other people's trauma; it's their baggage and their issues. She doesn't learn because she doesn't think she needs to learn anything.

The Bad Bitch self-reflects to become more self-aware. She traces herself back to recognize how her old wounds are showing up reactively in that moment. She takes a pause to adjust how she would respond better next time. She vows to follow through on her change.

Instead of learning to face her triggers, the Good Girl believes that making more money or gaining more significance will fix it all.

THE GOOD GIRL BECOMES A BROKE SELF-MADE MILLIONAIRE

A self-acclaimed millionaire female entrepreneur reached out to me for a conversation.

At first, she wanted to develop a friendship. She said that she's always had trouble with female friendships and becoming a successful entrepreneur made her more lonely. She wanted to make friends with women who were "at her level."

After two conversations, each lasting an hour and a half, I quickly realized that she needed to become a client because what she needed from me was beyond the scope of a friendship. She had a really bad case of a scarcity mindset that she needed to resolve.

Following our conversations, she sent me many long audio messages about her problems. I told her that she needed to work with me as a client, as we were venturing into a territory where we were not able to give each other equal value as friends.

She was not happy with my honesty. She wanted my validation, not to be directed to look at herself with honesty.

To cope with her insecurity, she came at me with "I'm better than you, look what I've done."

What she had done had little net merit.

She had initially built her business to over a million dollars in revenue. From this place, she made many hiring and business-decision mistakes, where she overspent her budget with redundant high expenses and overpaid her staff without guiding them with proper leadership.

When personal life issues arose in her life, which took her away from being the center of the business, her business completely crumbled. Her decision-making style was clearly based on fear, fight-or-flight, and dysregulated reactiveness.

As her business dwindled, her million-dollar revenue disappeared to hit $0.

When she reached out to me for friendship, she was starting to build it up again. She told me that she just needed to make more money. She couldn't see that the business was only a reflection of her inner being. She believed that all she had to do was to make more money, as she had done before.

She believed that her broken business results had nothing to do with her mindset issues.

She did not realize that the lack of true friendships, her inability to maintain and grow a business, and wanting free and unlimited conversations to fix her most important problems, were only signs and symptoms of her mindset issues, the root cause of what kept driving her to experience recurring pains in her life.

You can already see where she'll end up again with her scarcity mindset decision-making. As long as she refuses to look at herself in the mirror, she'll keep repeating the same problem over and over again.

Every human has a stubborn abundance-scarcity scale thermostat. Our childhood environment sets up the standard, and that's the standard where we keep going back. More money doesn't recalibrate the thermostat. More money simply amplifies the scale of the impact.

70% of lottery winners go bankrupt an average of 3-5 years after winning. Their scarcity mindset has no end. It's an urn with a cracked bottom. They buy non-stop, or put their money where it doesn't grow, until they're back to their default state on their thermostat.

The Good Girl attempts to outwit the scarcity mindset by seeking more wealth and significance, but the scarcity mindset grows greater in correlation to her wealth. It eventually becomes so big that it consumes and controls her in the form of greed, tyranny, and entitlement, causing her to sink even deeper into the black hole of despair and doom.

If you're realizing that you've had these similar experiences, this is where you have to overcome yourself. In the midst of the triggers that you may be feeling now for being "called out," you have to allow your own wisdom to peek through. Commit to change. Be resilient to face whatever you need to face.

Just as the Good Girl gets triggered, the Bad Bitch does too. Triggers never go away. Growth is progressively forever. There will always be the next level, and the next level always comes with a set of triggers to untangle.

Triggers feel like electrocution. Only *you* feel it, and what triggers you is highly individual, as these triggers are formed based on your past pains: wounds involving loss, judgment, abandonment, and rejection. It's a very intense feeling where you have no control over the pain that takes over every cell of your body within milliseconds. You feel paralyzed. Your logical thinking disappears. Your primitive survival coping mechanism takes over. You may get an insight during these moments where you feel like you're suddenly a child again; for example, feeling like you're five years old.

In this moment, the Good Girl automatically reacts as she always has done, but the Bad Bitch takes a breath, a moment of silence, and creates space between the impulsive reaction and herself. This moment allows for her to stop her default reaction in its tracks, and instead, chooses a different response.

This is what's required of you to outwit the scarcity mindset.

The Good Girl invests in momentary comfort, whereas the Bad Bitch invests in her future. She lives an abundant life because she faces herself.

In the moment when you're triggered, your primitive emotions take over and you can't find your logical footing. The Bad Bitch finds the inner strength to pause and ask herself, "What do I want to achieve from this situation?"

She focuses on that outcome and chooses a response that fits into her agenda: "How do I need to respond in this situation to..."

- ♦ Create better financial returns in the long term?
- ♦ Return more value for the money?
- ♦ Create a higher quality of life and connection with my loved ones?

This is the moment that changes your life. This is self-control. This is emotional management.

This is why the Bad Bitch excels in decision-making.

This is how the Bad Bitch invests in the right helpful people, maintains her stellar reputation, and is an excellent financial earner *and* manager.

To do this, you have to *feel safe*. You can't outwit the scarcity mindset unless you teach yourself to feel inner peace in moments of stress and conflict.

Abundance mindset begins when you embody safety.

In the Subconscious Reprogramming chapter, you'll remember that the third step to manifesting through the subconscious reprogramming process is to *cultivate safety*. All manifestations and abundance embodiments start here.

How to teach yourself to embody safety:

1. Sit with yourself without any distractions, preferably in a dark room in a comfortable setting.

2. Allow yourself to feel and notice your emotions.

3. Find the part of your body where you feel emotional discomfort. Put your hands on that part of your body to create focus.

4. While focusing on that body part, use concise language to articulate your thoughts and name your feelings, which gives an identity to the fears that control your decision-making.

5. Ask yourself what past experiences these fears stem from.

6. Thank your body for sharing this knowledge, and help yourself choose aligned thoughts that help you feel peace and calm.

7. Focus on that feeling while you feel grounded in the seat of your body, and experience complete relaxation and peace.

8. Repeat the exercise as a part of your daily routine, once in the morning, and once in the evening, or at least once a day.

When you feel peace and calm in your body, you start projecting abundance. Your energy creates a magnetic field for abundance that attracts the right people and opportunities.

As you release fear, you release control. You become pleasant and wonderful to deal with.

Successful people resonate with your energy and want to connect, collaborate, and help you.

As you experience peace, you start evaluating the relationships and habits you've been holding onto that do not resonate with this standard.

You let go of low vibrational habits, the attachment to struggle, and anxiety-inducing relationships. This is where you set appropriate boundaries to help yourself maintain your abundant state.

In this state, you make sound decisions that build and sustain abundance.

From the state of peace, you recognize when what appears as a lucrative offer is out of alignment with your integrity and long-term goals. Decision-making is simple when you know what you want. You say "No," to what doesn't align, and you know you made the right choice because you feel at peace.

This is the abundance mindset and where surviving ends and thriving begins.

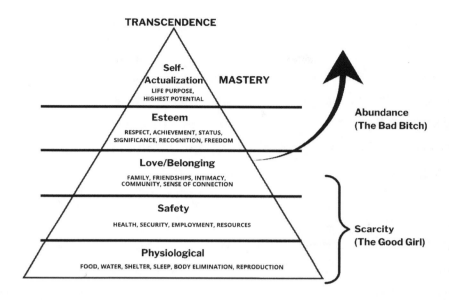

Maslow's Hierarchy of Needs With Additional Notes

In Maslow's Hierarchy of Needs, this is the stage where you've resolved the third tier, Love and Belonging, and have reached the fourth tier, Self-Esteem. This is where you feel safe as you build lasting and sustainable merit, significance, achievement, and respect.

This is where your growth takes on exponential speed. It's only a matter of time and effort on this pathway to Mastery, to reach your highest potential, becoming the most that you can be, which is the top tier of Maslow's pyramid, Self-Actualization.

THIS BAD BITCH TURNED DOWN $1 MILLION

In the early 1990s, singer-songwriter Jewel Kilcher was offered a contract by a record label that would have given her $1 million. At the time, she was barely making ends meet, playing music in a coffee shop, and living in her car.

She was really excited. Finally, her struggling artist days seemed to be over.

However, the more she dived deep into the contract, she realized that this $1 million was going to cost her artistry and creative control. The label wanted her to conform to a more pop-oriented sound that didn't align with her artistic vision.

To the surprise of everyone and even herself, she chose to turn down the offer.

This made no logical sense. She was living in scarcity. She got an offer that most music artists never get. This could have been her one and only and her last chance to get a record deal.

Jewel stuck to her vision and continued her coffee shop performances. She was already experiencing rising local fame when the company offered her the record deal.

Her decision to decline the misaligned offer had a counter-logical effect: it increased her self-belief and clarified her artistic vision.

Her local popularity skyrocketed even more. It was typical for her performances to create a huge lineup down the sidewalk.

Jewel's decision to decline the contract was a bold move that showcased her commitment to her authenticity and artistic integrity. Instead of compromising her musical style for a quick financial gain from a place of a scarcity mindset, she chose to stay true to her folk-influenced sound and heartfelt songwriting that was true to her story and her experiences.

This abundant mindset decision set the tone for her career and laid the foundation for her eventual greater success as a singer-songwriter.

By staying true to herself and her artistic vision, Jewel experienced lasting international fame and multi-million-dollar success that most folk artists don't get to experience.

Based on her loyal fanbase, she eventually signed a record deal that allowed her to create the music she wanted with her debut album, *Pieces of You.*

Taking the initial $1 million as a tradeoff to losing her creative control wouldn't have ever resulted in her long-term success. This would have been scarce decision-making, a decision only good for momentary survival. A scarce decision leads to scarce outcomes.

Jewel's decision to choose her artistry over temporary money was about keeping her integrity, which was an abundant decision. Preserving her artistic integrity has proven paramount to her, as it has not only upheld her devoted, long-term fanbase but also played a pivotal role in her enduring success.

CHAPTER FIFTEEN

Mastermind to Mastery

One Bad Bitch's success takes a village.

The Good Girl gets whipped by the forces of her environment. Her problem isn't only her willpower. Her environment doesn't allow her to thrive.

She gets controlled and taken off course.

Even when she achieves a certain level of success, she loses it as quickly as it came in.

Having the wrong people around her means that her life is full of drama. She's bombarded with a constant series of distractions and complex interpersonal problems that aren't even her issues, but she feels obligated to help so she can be seen as Good.

You're pulled away from doing your life's work.

You can't let go of people, lowering yourself to maintain relationships that have long expired.

You keep allowing in demeaning family members and old friends who don't get your growth, who keep trivializing your dreams and efforts.

In this environment, you aren't challenged to improve your competence in skills, your leadership, and your mindset, so you coast in the status quo.

If you become too successful, they might hate you. Staying small helps you meet the relationship standards in your current environment.

You live a mediocre life because this environment isn't the right pathway to reach Mastery.

The Good Girl is a lone wolf. While this makes sense when starting out in your journey, there is only so much you can do to help yourself when sorely relying on yourself and your own perspective.

The Bad Bitch's success is much more nuanced than what it looks to the outside world.

Every Bad Bitch has an excellently curated ecosystem with the right support system.

Observe her life in detail, and she didn't make her success alone.

She had the right community.

HER FAMILY MADE THIS BAD BITCH A MEGASTAR

It was obvious that from a very young age, Beyoncé Knowles had a passion and talent for singing and performing.

Both of her parents immediately nurtured her talent and supported her early career in the music industry. She was given lessons. Her father trained her to become a star performer. He allegedly made her practice moving gracefully in heels by teaching her to run on a moving treadmill with high heels on. Her mother took care of her performance fashion, makeup, and hair. Her parents provided her with opportunities to showcase her skills.

Her whole family revolved around making Beyoncé's dream career come true. Her father quit a six-figure job to become her full-time manager, betting himself on his daughter's career, where most people fail without seeing any tangible results.

Beyoncé's father, Mathew, played a significant role in her career as her manager during her time with Destiny's Child, an all-girl group that propelled Beyoncé to fame in the late 1990s and early 2000s. Her mother, Tina, was the costume designer and made sure that everyone looked beautiful and shining on stage. Both parents provided a lot of encouragement and moral support.

While Beyoncé's musical prowess, dynamic performances, and powerful vocals have earned her a prominent place in the music industry, everyone, including Beyoncé, knows that she wouldn't be where she is if it wasn't for her family and her community who fought every inch of the steps to her stardom.

You may think, "I'm not Beyoncé. I don't have a family supporting me, and I don't have any community that I can get support from."

Having a family like Beyoncé's is rarer than winning the lottery. You don't even need a whole family. If you have one parent who saw you for who you are and helped you hone your talent, then that's like you've won the lottery.

It's a lottery because the environment you're born into isn't something you can choose. Most people have families who undervalue them and don't acknowledge their talents and skills. It's a lottery because it's "nice to have" but most people don't get to have it.

Even when you're born into a supportive family, it's not a 100% foolproof lifetime guarantee. Tejana singer Selena Quintanilla had a similar family to Beyoncé. However, according to the version of her story that was approved by her family, she and her family did not pay close attention to the quality of the people in her inner circle. At the cusp of peaking in her stardom, Selena was tragically murdered by Yolanda Saldívar, the president of her fan club and a so-called close friend.

Britney Spears is another example of having a family that launched her to stardom, but according to her, they also broke her. Singer Mariah Carey is grateful for her mother's influence that helped her recognize her talent, but also speaks of needing hard boundaries with her family as she became world-famous.

People around you matter. They make or break your success. Your environment has immense power over you, but that willpower alone can't make you succeed.

Having a family that supports you is a rare case. These stories only show you that nobody makes it alone and how many people actually have to come together to have one shining Bad Bitch success story.

This Bad Bitch Succeeded Without Family (But Not on Her Own)

If you can't relate to Beyoncé and Selena, you still have no excuses because you can shift your lens and look at someone like Rihanna.

Rihanna came from poverty and a lot of domestic abuse. She was born in Barbados, where there are fewer opportunities than in the US. RiRi is a real Bad Bitch. She found her strength as a singer and performer early on and laser-focused. She invested time and energy into her craft.

Although Rihanna doesn't talk very much in detail about her early days, it's obvious that she had a vision and kept it. She likely sought out people who could help her hone that vision into reality. There were too many things in her environment that would have been threats to her ambition. For example, she was born into a culture where getting married and having babies early was an expected norm for girls. In an environment where economic safety isn't easily viable, choosing a realistic job is also an expectation.

Based on her condition, Rihanna had all the reasons to have a default life and settle, but she didn't. She needed people who could at least validate her dreams, whether they were people who told her she was talented, saw her as a star, or actually had industry knowledge and connections.

She was 16 years young when she put herself in front of a producer, who connected her to Jay-Z. Most 16-year-olds can't even make a speech in front of their teacher and peers. Imagine what it took for a 16-year-old Rihanna to dare to believe that she's meant to be a star. She didn't cook that up and maintain that perspective in her head, all alone, in the midst of her family's domestic violence and financial struggles.

Every successful person has somebody and continues to have somebody that supports them.

Nobody makes it alone.

An average Bad Bitch does not come from a supportive family, just like most self-made millionaires didn't win the lottery. They made it happen with their own mindset and efforts, leveraging the right types of people and networks.

What is indisputable is that you need the right people to succeed. If you observe any successful person, the secret to their success is that they branched out and found their community.

You always need someone who believes in you more than you do.

An average Bad Bitch is far from being average because she finds a solution to this.

She finds herself in a Mastermind group. This stellar community keeps her humble, creative, and inspired to create more. This is the community that polishes that diamond in the rough into a sparkling gem.

EVEN A BAD BITCH PRODIGY NEEDS A VILLAGE

Misty Copeland was a thirteen-year-old African American girl who started taking ballet lessons at the local Boys and Girls Club. She came from a single mom family with little money. She experienced love at first sight with ballet.

Even though thirteen is a very old age to start ballet training as a professional, even without any previous dance training, Misty excelled in it to the level that her teacher, Cynthia Bradley, couldn't help but notice Misty's outstanding talent.

Within just a few months of starting ballet, Misty was en pointe, which is the kind of progress timeline that is unheard of in the ballet world. Aspiring dancers start dancing at preschool age, and devote years to rigorous training and physical conditioning before they can even begin to dance en pointe during their teenage years.

As Misty became very involved in ballet, it started to become an inconvenience to her family. Her mother faced time issues with driving Misty to and from lessons, rehearsals, and other ballet-related activities. The finances were the other concern. Ballet is a high-brow art form, and becoming serious in it costs a lot of money. Misty's mother wanted her daughter to stop dancing for these reasons.

That's when Cynthia stood up and convinced Misty's mother that this girl was born to dance and that she needed to keep dancing. She asked to become Misty's guardian so she could help her meet all the training needs. Misty ended up moving in with Cynthia.

Misty's mother didn't seem to understand the importance of ballet. There was alleged jealousy and conflict between her mother and Cynthia. Misty continued to dance despite the adversity with her family, with the support of her teacher and many strangers who believed in her more than she often believed in herself. At the time, there were almost no black role models in the professional ballet world. Misty never saw anyone who looked like her while training for her ambition.

In 2015, Misty Copeland became the first African-American principal dancer in American Ballet Theatre, the first in ABT's 75-year history.

Since then, Misty has become a celebrity beyond the ballet world as a public speaker, author, and influencer. One of her most notable commercial campaigns was with Under Armour, where her story of resilience, endurance, and grace successfully promoted their activewear while sending an uplifting message of self-worth, especially for those who belong in marginalized and underprivileged communities.

Misty didn't have the right family, but her community was behind her success.

This Bad Bitch's Elite Community Made Her a Success

You may think that Misty was lucky enough to have met her ballet teacher, but you didn't.

Your community is your chosen family, and you can look for them.

Gabrielle "Coco" Chanel was born into a poor family in Saumur, France, in the late 19th century. She grew up in a low-class environment with very scarce resources. At 11, upon her mother's death, her father sent her to live at a convent.

She learned to sew from the nuns. Despite her impoverished upbringing with no formal education, she possessed a keen sense of design. In her early years, she worked as a seamstress and cabaret singer, which provided her with exposure to various elite social circles.

She was a captivating and charismatic woman who knew how to make lasting impressions on influential individuals. Early in her career, she formed relationships with wealthy and influential men, such as Étienne Balsan and Arthur "Boy" Capel, who provided financial support and connections that enabled her to launch her fashion business.

With her refined social skills, she navigated the elite circles of Parisian high society. She was admired for her wit, charm, and unique style, which allowed her to befriend actresses, artists, and members of the aristocracy.

Her innate understanding of what women wanted in clothing, paired with these connections, helped her gain a foothold in the world of fashion and provided her with the opportunity to showcase her designs to the influential women of the time.

Her designs were groundbreaking, as during this time, women were still struggling in tight Victorian corsets. Inspired by menswear, she introduced simple garments, a typical set involving a cardigan and a pleated skirt, with a low-belted pullover top made of jersey (wool knit) fabric. She was also the first designer to introduce trousers in womenswear. Her fashion designs lifted the garment oppression women were suffering from with the tight corsets and impractical and complicated dresses that made movement very difficult for women. The high society women quickly became obsessed and addicted to Coco's designs.

Her talent, combined with her networking skills, propelled her to establish her eponymous fashion brand, Chanel. Coco Chanel revolutionized women's fashion by introducing practical yet elegant designs, such as the iconic little black dress, tweed suits, and the now-famous Chanel No. 5 perfume. Her creations resonated with women, and her brand quickly became synonymous with luxury and sophistication.

There could have never been Coco Chanel or the Chanel brand that is synonymous with class, high society, and elegance without her ability to connect with aristocracy and high society, the right community that propelled her and her brand to high status, which took her ambition to reach her greatest potential.

You may be thinking that if you could have the types of success mentioned here, your life would be problem free, but that's not true.

Your initial success is only the beginning.

As you rise, your challenges change, and that's why you need the right people.

With success and wealth, you feel powerful. It is only human nature to become pompous, righteous, self-indulgent, and to stop listening to feedback.

Power can contaminate the once humble mind with the Golden Child Syndrome, where you believe that you were chosen and, therefore, are somewhat invincible.

This mindset blocks your growth. You keep trying to do the same thing you've always done. You stop growing.

People fall for the Golden Child bias at their peak all the time, and companies do too.

Kodak once dominated the film photography industry but did not catch on with the rise of digital photography. They were the Golden Child of film photography. What people don't know is that Kodak's engineer, Steven Sasson, was the first to invent the first digital camera in 1975, almost 30 years before it became hugely popularized in the market to become the world standard.

Instead of embracing change to continuously dominate, Kodak resisted. They buried the invention.

No doubt there were many in the company who saw the need for change, but the decision-makers were not open to this change. After decades of dominance, Kodak fell behind in the industry and declared bankruptcy in 2012.

Winning back-to-back can create an inflated sense of self, which becomes a dangerous threat that leads to self-sabotage.

The Bad Bitch is wise. She knows that success is not a destination.

She understands that if she doesn't manage her mind carefully at the peak of her success, she'll drive herself back to a scarcity mindset and sabotage herself to her detriment.

This is how a win can abruptly, and quickly, turn into a losing streak.

This is why the Bad Bitch does risk management with her own mind, why she needs the right people who keep her in check, and why she needs a well-curated Mastermind.

A Mastermind is a community that:

- Challenges you.
- Keeps you humble.
- Opens you up to new ideas, strategies, and possibilities.
- Raises your standards.
- Keeps you accountable.
- Elevates you to a network of new opportunities.

This is her inner circle, composed of those who are more successful and accomplished than her in their area of expertise, including a mindset expert.

This is her company of counsel.

The Bad Bitch has skilled advisors to help her get back on track when her sense of self is influenced negatively.

Her people are self-sufficient, business savvy experts who have their needs met, who are driven and focused, and collaborate with value.

She is surrounded by mature, accomplished professionals, which create the standard to continuously improve their competence to reach Mastery.

They are dedicated to improving their mindset and leadership skills.

The Bad Bitch knows that *people* take her to higher grounds.

She also knows that at every stage of success, there are new challenges she can't face alone.

She knows she's forced to experience the most growth when she experiences loss, failures, and hardship. She's always ready for a new opportunity to experience radical growth.

Only diamonds can sharpen and polish diamonds. This is why every elite and powerful family values their network.

Those born wealthy know the value of creating and maintaining powerful and successful connections, while those born poor or middle class who spent time acquiring money spend most of their time cultivating skills and seeking opportunities.

Networking is playing a long-term game, while hustling for opportunities is short-term success.

The right network is why wealthy people have a leisurely life, while the rest hustle. It's how a millionaire can lose everything but their connections and still come out on top.

Unless you network well on your pathway to acquiring wealth and success, you'll be forever stuck in hustle mode.

This is why the Bad Bitch sets the right intention from the beginning.

Your Bad Bitch Era is a Mastery lifestyle, backed by her trusted Mastermind:

1. You're highly focused and are specific.

2. Your most important tasks are done first thing in the day, without distractions.

3. Your life is organized and spontaneous with the purpose of being highly effective.

4. You have almost everything delegated, especially house chores and menial tasks.

5. You have very few people in your circle, but they all collaborate to be high-producing and effective.

6. You have excellent people on speed dial if you get stuck on something.

7. You have a daily healing mindset routine.

8. You eat the most nourishing foods to fuel your energy.

9. You prioritize fitness and self-care because your health is what manifests abundance.

10. You exude achievement, courage, leadership, and power.

11. The work you do is highly inspiring, life-giving, and purposeful.

12. Your legacy and long-term plan visions drive you to show up every single day.

The more focused, outspoken, and driven you are by your conviction, the more you shine. The Mastery life is what emanates the energy to attract the right people to collaborate, help, and open doors to make it happen.

When you're surrounded by quality people, diamond polishes diamond. Your network becomes the centrifugal force that mutually lifts you and your community into an upward spiral.

You've likely heard you're the sum of the five people you spend the most time with, and you've already seen it in action. Where would Madam C.J. Walker be without Annie? Where would Misty Copeland be without her first ballet teacher, Cynthia Bradley, who went out of her way to nurture Misty's raw talent? Where would Sara Blakely be if she never reached someone who could get her on Oprah?

When you follow the Bad Bitch formula outlined in this book and align yourself with the right people, the impossible happens and miracles become real.

Time compresses, where goals that should have taken you years can come together within weeks or months.

When channeled and used right, your mindset, energy, focus, and resourcefulness, with collaboration with the right community, you reach your highest potential.

You Self-Actualize.

As you enter your Bad Bitch Era, you want to consider an inner circle that takes this lifestyle to the next level. We're talking about a Mastermind that's not just any group, but a curated, exclusive community of like-minded individuals. This is where the real magic happens. We're not opening the doors often and spots are limited. So, if you're serious about your journey, you'd be in good company with us.

Take the first step towards something extraordinary. Curious?

Check out **www.juliacha.com/Bad-Bitch-On-Top** to find out more.

This isn't something you want to miss. This isn't just an opportunity; it's your lifeline to leveling up in ways you've only dreamed of. Take the leap. Someday never comes while you're waiting, so that means the perfect moment is now.

Find out your advantages, learn to play your cards right, and build elite networks and connections. Look around you. Is your circle of people lifting you up or pulling you down?

Your inner Bad Bitch knows the answer.

Your success, your mindset, and your future are too important to wait on and to leave to chance. You could be one connection away from skyrocketing your success. So ask yourself: How can you afford *not* to have a Mastermind in your pursuit of Mastery?

Make the conscious choice to surround yourself with those who not only dream of greatness, but actively pursue it.

This is You On Top.

Welcome to your Bad Bitch Era.

Your Era

Don't forget to join our community: www.juliacha.com/Bad-Bitch-On-Top

Follow Julia on social media to get free and instant coaching:

TikTok: https://www.tiktok.com/@juliajcha

Instagram: https://www.instagram.com/juliajcha/

YouTube: https://youtube.com/juliacha

LinkedIn: https://www.linkedin.com/in/juliacha/

Facebook: https://www.facebook.com/juliajcha

Made in the USA
Columbia, SC
06 December 2023

27887958R00089